AF361455

THE JUDICIAL INTERROGATION
OF THE PARTIES

A HISTORICAL SYNOPSIS
AND A COMMENTARY

The Catholic University of America
Canon Law Studies
No. 269

THE JUDICIAL INTERROGATION OF THE PARTIES

A Historical Synopsis and a Commentary

BY

REV. ROBERT B. CLUNE, B.A., J.C.L.
Priest of the Archdiocese of Toronto

A DISSERTATION

SUBMITTED TO THE FACULTY OF THE SCHOOL OF CANON LAW OF THE
CATHOLIC UNIVERSITY OF AMERICA IN PARTIAL FULFILLMENT
OF THE REQUIREMENTS FOR THE DEGREE OF
DOCTOR OF CANON LAW

The Catholic University of America Press
Washington, D.C.
1948

NIHIL OBSTAT:

JOANNES ROGG SCHMIDT, A.B. J.C.D.
Censor Deputatus,
Washingtonii, die I iunii, 1948.

IMPRIMATUR:

✠JACOBUS C. CARDINAL McGUIGAN, D.D.,
Archiepiscopus Torontinus,
Toronto, die 5 iunii, 1948.

PRINTED BY
THE MISSION PRESS,
67 BOND STREET,
TORONTO, CANADA

TO THE BLESSED MOTHER

TABLE OF CONTENTS

CHAPTER VII

CHAPTER VIII

FOREWORD

"Whenever a sense of equity influences a judge, there is no doubt that in the pursuance of justice an interrogatory should take place."[1] Thus wrote Ulpian, a great classical jurist of Roman Law, whose works alone comprise almost one-third of the *Digest* of Justinian.

The truth of this statement is practically self-evident. It follows as a logical consequence that, when matter for adjudication is brought before a person acting in the capacity of a judge, certain questions must be asked of the parties and their witnesses before it can be said that the judge fully understands the case and can arrive at a just and equitable decision. Thus it is not so much the fact of interrogation which is the chief concern of this dissertation, but primarily the method or the procedural element of this phase of the trial.

The strictly judicial interrogation is that which is exercised with the exact observance of all the essential formalities of legal procedure. To understand rightly what are judicial and what are extra-judicial acts, it is necessary to know exactly what is a *iudicium*. Not everything that a judge does is a judicial act, but only that which he does *in iudicio*. The Code of Canon Law, in canon 1552, § 1, gives this description of a *iudicium*—the legitimate discussion and settlement of a controversy in a matter over which the Church has the right of examination before an ecclesiastical tribunal. All the parts of the description are essential, and one must consider them all when treating of the judicial interrogation of the parties.

Although the interrogation of the parties and that of the witnesses have much in common, the scope of the present study will be limited, in so far as it is possible, to that of the parties.

---

[1] D. (11,1), 21.—Scott, *The Civil Law*, a Translation of the Code of Justinian (14 vols., The Civil Trust Co., Philadelphia, 1932), IV, 68.

The term ''parties'' includes the plaintiff and the defendant, while those who may be brought forward to substantiate or to give information regarding the claims of one or the other of the parties are called witnesses.

While a confession, or the ceding on the part of one litigant to the claims of the adverse party, constitutes a proof of the truth of the opponent's position, it may or may not be considered by the ecclesiastical law as constituting full proof.[2] Consequently, even in the case of a confession, it remains necessary to question the parties closely as to their respective claims and the proofs which they can produce to verify their contentions.

The writer wishes to express his sincere gratitude to His Eminence James Cardinal McGuigan, Archbishop of Toronto, for the opportunity to pursue advanced studies at the Catholic University of America, and to the members of the Faculty of the School of Canon Law for their profitable instruction and kind assistance.

-----

[2]Canons 1751, 1747, n. 3.

PART I

HISTORICAL CONSPECTUS .

THE JUDICIAL INTERROGATION OF THE PARTIES IN
ROMAN LAW

Article 1. Roman Civil Law Procedure

In the historical development of Roman Law there are to be found, apart from differences of detail, three distinct systems of procedure: the *Legis Actio,* the Formulary System and the *Cognito Extraordinaria.* The periods during which these systems were in use overlapped, but broadly it may be said that the system of the *Legis Actio* prevailed until the passing of the *Lex Aebutia,* probably in the second half of the second century B.C.; that of the Formulary System was chiefly used from the last century of the Republic until the end of the Classical Period (3rd century); and that of the *Cognitio Extraordinaria* was in use in the post-classical times.

In the first two systems there were no strict rules of procedure to be followed as to the interrogation of the parties. After the dispute had been brought to the attention of the magistrate by the plaintiff and the defendant had appeared, the nature of the suit was determined and a judge or arbiter was chosen with the consent of both parties. This part of the proceedings was called *"in iure."*

The parties then appeared before the judge, and thus the procedure continued *"apud iudicem."* These proceedings before the judge seem also to have been, from the earliest times, free from the restriction of form.[1] There were, however, certain rules of evidence that had to be followed, and these served to point out, in a limited way, the progress that the Romans were making in their efforts to arrive at a just and equitable

---

[1]H. F. Jolowicz, *Historical Introduction to the Study of Roman Law* (Cambridge University Press, 1932), p. 186.

1

procedure. Among these rules were the following, namely, that the burden of proof rested upon the plaintiff,[2] and that the judge had to hear both parties, unless one party did not appear by midday and had no valid excuse.[3]

It seems that the essential difference between these two systems was the discretionary power vested in the magistrate. In the *Legis Actio*, the magistrate supervised the appointment of an arbiter, but in the Formulary System the magistrate embodied the issues at stake in a formula which limited the future proceedings *"apud iudicem"* to the claims contained therein. It was the duty of the parties to see that the dispute was stated correctly. The acceptance of the formula by the defendant constituted the beginning of that part of the trial which was called the "joining of issue."

Under the Formulary System there were certain actions which received the name of *"Actiones Interrogatoriae."* These actions were typified by the fact that the plaintiff, before settling the exact grounds of his suit, could question the defendant as to the circumstances which affected not only liability in general, but his personal liability in the matter to be litigated. This occurred in noxal actions, when it was necessary to determine the *"potestas"* of a defendant over some slave who had caused harm to another. This *"Interrogatio in iure,"* as it was called, also took place in action against the heir of a debtor. The plaintiff asked whether and for what share the defendant was heir. This was an important question, since also the liabilities were divided among the heirs.

There was, to be sure, nothing unusual in permitting the plaintiff to question his opponent. But the interrogations of these actions evinced a special institution. Its peculiarity was twofold. In the first place, the person questioned was bound by his answers, and in the second, if he refused to answer, or if he answered uncertainly, the plaintiff could proceed as though his opponent had answered by stating a fact which was favorable to his, the plaintiff's, suit.

---

[2] D. (22, 3) 2.
[3] Tables, 1, 7.

When, in the ensuing action, the plaintiff proceeded on the basis of the fact thus admitted, and this fact, for his benefit, was set forth in the formula as drawn up by the magistrate to form the "joinder of issue," there existed what was known as the *"Actio Interrogatoria."*

It may be noted, then, that in actions of this kind the plaintiff possessed the right to question his opponent, and that this right entailed the corresponding obligation of the defendant to answer truthfully. The magistrate had no authority to question either party, but it was his duty to take cognizance of these questions and answers in the drawing up of the formula which defined the claims of the parties. It was this formula which governed the proceedings *"apud iudicem."*

As Roman Law procedure developed, however, into the system known as the *"Cognitio Extraordinaria,"* the right of the plaintiff to question the defendant as to his personal liability was done away with, for as Callistratus, a Roman jurist, had stated, "No one can be compelled to answer anything with refernce to his rights before the case is tried, and therefore this type of judicial action is of rare if at all continued occurrence." Callistratus further remarked, "that only matters stated by the adverse party in the presence of the judge can be employed as proof by the litigants, whether such matters relate to estates or to the other things involved in the judicial proceedings."[4] Thus the special significance of the *"Interrogationes in iure"* had disappeared, and the interrogations served simply for the establishing of evidence or of proof.

In this later form of procedure, namely the *"Cognitio Extraordinaria"* which superseded the Formulary System in the third century, the outstanding change apart from differences of detail was the foregoing of the reference of the case from the magistrate to the judge; the *"ordo iudiciorum"* was gone, and the whole matter was tried by the magistrate or his deputy. The magistrate, had, of course, to abide by the law, but nevertheless he controlled the entire procedure.

---

[4]D. (11, 1) 1.

After the summons had been issued by the magistrate on the complaint of the plaintiff, the parties appeared in court on the appointed day, and stated their case and the facts upon which they relied. If the defendant acknowledged the justice of the claim, then the judgment was given against him. This was the Roman *"Confessio in iure."* If he did not confess, then after the aforementioned statement of the parties an oath, the *"iuramentum calumniae,"* was tendered to the parties. In it they stated that they were not acting vexatiously.[5] the case was then argued by the advocates of the parties to its ultimate conclusion.

Once the class of actions known as the *"Actiones Interrogatoriae"* had disappeared from use, the interrogations themselves became even more important. In any action and at any stage either party could submit an interrogation to the other, by leave of and through the judge.[6] The judge also was definitely instructed to ask questions of the parties in order to arrive at as complete as possible an understanding of the matter in question.[7]

In the *Digest* of Justinian there are to be found many rules and examples regarding the interrogation of the parties. Though these writings were from the pens of men who lived and wrote during the classical period of Roman law, and who consequently lived during the era of the Formulary System, the fact that these writings were quoted in the *Digest* tended to show that they were regarded as illustrating essential principles of procedure irrespective of the system in use at the time. For as Buckland says, "the compilers were to alter the original texts so as to make them state current law."[8]

It is for this reason that these texts have been considered at this point in the historical survey, rather than under the Formulary System, with reference to which the *"Actiones Interrogatoriae"* were treated. For, while many of the texts

---

[5] C. (2, 58) 2; C. (3, 1) (14, 4).

[6] Buckland, *A Text-Book of Roman Law from Augustus to Justinian* (2. ed., Cambridge: The Cambridge University Press, 1932), p. 666.

[7] C. (3, 1) 9; C. Th. (2, 18) 1.

[8] Buckland, *op. cit.*, p. 42.

may have been applicable at that time, it is still not certain that they were. But that they did apply during the later period of Roman Law is definitely certain.

In the *Digest*, then, are found the following points of interest most of which are self-explanatory.[9]

a) Gaius on the Provincial Edicts.

When anyone was interrogated whether he was an heir, to what portion of the estate he was entitled, or whether he had under his control anyone on whose account a noxal action was brought, he was to be afforded time for deliberation, since if he made an incorrect statement he became subjected to inconvenience.[10]

b) Ulpianus on the Edict.

Sometimes a person was not compelled to answer when he was interrogated whether he was an heir, as, for instance, when he was sued by another in the event that the estate was in dispute (and this was determined by the divine Hadrian), for otherwise, if he denied that he was the heir, he might become entangled in such a way as to be deprived of his estate.[11]

It was left to the discretionary power of the judge to decide whether a person could be compelled to answer incriminating questions of this type. If the judge decided in favor of the defendant, then the question was disallowed; but if he decided otherwise, then the defendant had to answer to the question under the pain of being declared contumacious if he remained silent. Ulpianus had the following to say on this point.

c) Ulpianus on the Edict

When one kept silent in the presence of the praetor, his position was such that, if the action was brought against him, he could be sued for the entire amount, just as if he were the heir:

9D. (11, 1)—delineated as found in Scott, *The Civil Law*, a Translation of the Code of Justinian, IV, 68.

10D. (11, 1) 5.

11D. (11, 1) 6.

for when a person did not answer at all, he was to be considered as contumacious. He had to suffer the following penalty for his contumacy, that is to say, he could be sued for the entire amount, just as if he had denied that he was an heir, for then he was to be held as guilty of contempt of the praetor.[12]

d) Ulpianus on the Edict

When anyone without being interrogated nevertheless answered that he was the heir, it was deemed that an interrogation had been made. One had to consider the defendant as interrogated not only when the questions were asked by the praetor, but also when the same was done by the adversary.[13]

e) Ulpianus on the Edict

Sometimes a party when interrogated was required to answer also with reference to his age.[14]

f) Ulpianus on the Edict

Celsus had stated that party could recall his answer, if no disadvantage resulted to the plaintiff from his doing so; and this seemed perfectly allowable, especially if he did so after he had obtained from his friends more information as to his rights either through documents or by means of letters.[15]

It seems difficult to find an apt interpretation for the words, "if no disadvantage resulted to the plaintiff." For the defendant's withdrawing of his answer appeared not to offer him any advantage unless at the same time it occasioned a disadvantage for the plaintiff. Conversely stated, the rule would have implied that the defendant could withdraw only those statements which either did not affect the plaintiff's claims or proved simply advantageous to himself. For example, if Titus as defendant was the only heir, he alone was legally responsible for the claims against the estate. But what if he learned from

---

[12]D. (11, 1) (11, 5).
[13]D. (11, 1) 6.
[14]D. (11, 1) 11.
[15]D. (11, 1) (11, 12)

friends that his brother, of whom it was thought that he had perished, was still alive? Thus his brother existed as co-heir and became responsible for his share of the claims against the estate. Could Titus then withdraw his answer? Such a withdrawal no doubt worked to the disadvantage of the plaintiff, who in consequence could sue Titus for only one half of the original claim.

Equity seemed to demand that the defendant be allowed to withdraw his original statement. On the basis of the newly submitted evidence, it appeared to be the duty of the judge to rule in favor of the permissibility of withdrawing the previous statement.

Article 2. Roman Law Criminal Procedure

In the history of criminal procedure there existed three fundamental types i.e., the accusatory types, the inquisitorial types and the type which reflected elements incorporated from both of these. The criminal law of almost every nation has begun with the accusatory procedure, and this only later became changed to the inquisitorial procedure. To this general trend the Roman Law proved no exception. According to Esmein (1913),

> Roman criminal procedure, in accordance with the spirit of Roman criminal law and the ideas prevailing in Rome, was regularly based upon the principle of a formal accusation—not merely in the sense that only on the basis of a formal accusation could a criminal prosecution take place, but also in the sense that there was an issue only between the accuser and the accused, and that this issue was limited to the formal allegations of the accuser, who was obliged to furnish the evidence necessary for his case.[16]

Thus the State did not, in the pursuance of the public good, prosecute those who had committed an offense: this prosecution was left to the individual who had been wronged. The judge who could not proceed on his own initative, either in the taking of

---

[16]Esmein-Simpson, *A History of Continental Criminal Procedure* (Boston: Little, Brown & Co., 1913), p. 18.

jurisdiction or in the taking of evidence, merely examined the evidence placed before him and based his decision upon it. He was present as a second at a duel, in order to superintend the combat between the parties, and to see that it was fair throughout. If, in his opinion, the evidence was not sufficient to enable him to make an equitable decision, he could say, *"non liquet"*— the matter is not clear to me, and more evidence had to be presented.[17] The spirit of the accusatory system was that the burden of proof rested upon the accuser.

A few words should be said about the confession, which more often than not was the direct result of the interrogation of the party, particularly in criminal cases.

In the earlier period of Roman Law, nothing was calculated as a means for bringing about a confession. But in the event of a confession the accuser simply rested his case: he had no need of producing further evidence. There was at first no official examination of the truth of the confession.[18] Later, however, the reliability of a confession had to be substantiated with proof.

Under the Emperors, infringements which led to the destruction of civic freedom necessarily affected the old Roman criminal procedure. As the representative of the Emperor the judge was no longer limited to the use of the evidence brought before him. On his own initiative he could proceed to gather the evidence. In pursuance of this purpose he could interrogate both the parties and the witnesses.

Esmein stated further that at that period the confession of the accused as a means of proof acquired a new and preponderating influence. In the light of this fact the method *par excellence* for extracting such proof was torture. At first it was only to the slaves, and not to the citizens, that torture was applied. But in the early days of the Empire there arose the custom of subjecting to this process of examination the Roman citizen who stood accused of treason. "Then torture came to be of such

---

[17]Droste-Messmer, *Canonical Procedure in Disciplinary and Criminal Cases of Clerics* (New York, 1897), p. 82.

[18]Esmein-Simpson, *A History of Continental Criminal Procedure,* p. 24.

general application that the handbooks of the time recommend to the judges not to begin the examination by torture but, first, to collect the evidences.''[19]

In the Roman Law of the time of Justinian (527-565), however, certain qualities were demanded of the confession if it was to stand acceptable as proof. The person confessing had to be a major, that is, it was required that he have attained the age of twenty-five years; otherwise he could confess only on the authority of his guardian.[20]

Another requirement, as enacted by the Law of Justinian, was that the one who confessed had to be of sound mind, and that his confession was made not out of hatred or in the heat of anger. For anything that was said in the heat of anger was not considered of any effect, unless the very fact of the party's persevering adherence served to disclose the state of his mind.[21]

The confession also had to be such as to reflect disfavor upon the person who made it, for the Romans stated in their law that an unjust condition could not permissibly be imposed by one person upon another.[22] The confession also had to be made in the presence of the adversary or of his procurator. Lastly, the matter of the confession had to be such as not to imply what was impossible or palpably untrue. Thus, for instance, a person's confession could not command any credence if he asserted that he killed a certain man, when on the contrary it was a matter of public knowledge that the man was yet alive.[23]

---

[19]Esmein-Simpson, *op. cit.*, p. 9.

[20]D. (42, 2) (6, 5).

[21]D. (50, 17) 48.

[22]D. (50, 17) 74.

[23]D. (9, 2) 23, 1).

CHAPTER II

THE JUDICIAL INTERROGATION OF THE PARTIES FROM THE EARLY CENTURIES TO THE TIME OF GRATIAN

Article 1. Procedural Background of the Early Church

It was in the fourth century by the Edict of Milan (313) that the Church was freed from the fetters of persecution and permitted to emerge from the hidden recesses of the catacombs. Then, for the first time, the Church which had struggled so valiantly to preserve its very existence, had the opportunity to develop its own judicial procedure to handle those cases which were rightfully to fall within the scope of its own competence. But it should be noted that the first concern of the Church was the proper custody of the immense doctrinal deposit entrusted to its keeping. Such a question as that of a specifically demanded method of procedure in judicial matters, though an important one, was of much less weight, and thus was to look to a fuller development at a later date.

From the very beginning the Church had claimed the power to look into and to settle disputes that had arisen among its subjects. This is attested in many passages found in the New Testament, but more specifically in St. Paul's Epistle to the Corinthians.[1] In the same Epistle is reported St. Paul's act of judging the incestuous adulterer and of condemning him to the punishment of excommunication.[2]

Besides these passages of the New Testament, there are also various documents, as derived from tradition, which reveal the exercise of this judicial power and the beginning of a form of judicial procedure in the body ecclesiastic.[3]

---

[1] 1 Cor., 6, 1-8.

[2] I Cor., 5, 1-5.

[3] Tertullian, *Apologeticum*, cap. 39—Migne, *Patrologiae Cursus Completus—Series Latina* (221 vols., Parisiis, 1844-1855), I, col. 460 (hereafter cited as *MPL*). Cf. Ottaviani, *Institutiones Iuris Publici Ecclesiastici* (2. ed., 2 vols., Civitate Vaticana, 1935-1936), I, 237.

The Church, not having received a set of procedural norms from its Divine Founder, and yet from the very beginning instituting its own separate tribunals, in casting about for a form of procedure, naturally chose that with which it was the most familiar, namely, that which was used throughout the Empire in the secular courts. It must not be inferred, however, that the Roman method of procedure was adopted bodily just as it was. The Church, even in its infancy, adapted to its own needs what it borrowed from the Roman Law method of judicial procedure.[4]

That Roman Law was a supplementary source for the Ecclesiastical Law, in that sense that, when no specific disposition had been made by the Church authorities to cover a certain point, then the norm for action was the one which obtained in the civil law, is evidenced by Pope St. Gregory I (590-604), who ordered the rules of Roman Law procedure to be followed on points which were not regulated by the Ecclesiastical Laws.[5]

Though this seems to be the first official recognition of Roman Law as a subsidiary source in the ordering and shaping of canonical precedure, it merely confirmed a current practice of the ecclesiastical courts. For it is undeniable that a deep influence was exercised upon the procedural laws of the Church by Roman Law and, in particular, by the legislation as codified by Justinian.[6]

Article 2. The Judicial Interrogation of the Parties in the
Early Church

i. Legislation,

The fact that the Church used Roman Law as a supplementary source for its canonical procedure does much to

---

[4]Esmein-Simpson, *A History of Continental Criminal Procedure,* p. 78.

[5]*Gregorii I Papae Registrum Epistolarum,* Ep. XIII—*Montumenta Germaniae Historica, Epistolarum Tomus I et II* (edd. P. Ewald et L. Hartmann, Berolini; Apud Weidmannos, 1891-1899), I, 47.

[6]Benedetto Ojetti, "Ecclesiastical Courts"—*The Catholic Encyclopedia* (15 vols., Index and 2 Supplements, New York, 1907-1922), IV, 453; Droste-Messmer, *Canonical Procedure in the Disciplinary and Criminal Cases of Clerics,* p. 20.

explain the apparent lack of procedural rules with regard to the judicial interrogation of the parties. For generally the existing civil requirements were admirably suited to the Church's purpose.[7]

About the only clue that can be found in ecclesiastical literature, as indicating the canonical procedure to be followed in the matter of judicial interrogations, is the psuedo-Isidorian Decretal attributed to Pope St. Eleutherius (175-189), but which in reality seems to have been taken from the Theodosian Code.[8] In this pseudo-epistle are found the following instructions to the judges of the Ecclesiastical Province of Gaul. The judges were advised that they should examine diligently all the cases which were brought before their tribunals. The fact that they should interrogate the parties fully and frequently was clearly emphasized. That this should be done before the decision was rendered was another point that was set down as the norm to be followed in all processes.[9]

However this letter, which is so evidently a forgery, would be of little juridical value were it not for the fact that it was quoted many years later by Burchard of Worms (1012),[10] Ivo of Chartres (1090-1095),[11] and also by Gratian (ca. 1140),[12] as showing forth, in these later times, the mind of the Church regarding the judge's duty of interrogating the parties at trial along with their witnesses.

ii. The *Positiones*

At some time presumably during this period, a new element was introduced into the procedural law of the Church. It is not known at exactly what time, but Durantis (1238-1296) stated that the method of interrogation as mentioned by him

---

[7]Wanenmacher, *Canonical Evidence in Marriage Cases* (Philadelphia: The Dolphin Press, 1935), p. 50.

[8]*Codex Theodosianus* (ed. P. Kreuger, M. Mommsen, 3 vols., Berolini, 1905), (2.18), 1.

[9]Hinschius, *Decretales Pseudo-Isidorianae et Capitula Angilramni* (Lipsiae, 1863), p. 125.

[10]Burchard of Worms in Book XVI of his *Liber Decretorum—MPL.* CXL, col. 30.

[11]Ivo of Chartres, *Decretum*, Pars V—*MPL*, CLXI, 316, 317.

[12]C. 11, C. XXX, q. 5.

was of long standing.[13] While no indication of it obtained in the period preceding the decretalists, the method of interrogation to which they adverted was already an acknowledged form of procedure in their time.[14] This method pointed to the use of the so-called *positiones*.

In Germanic Law it was customary to subdivide the claims of the parties into distinct allegations, and it was necessary to prove each of these allegations as it had been formulated, otherwise the proof of the claim was considered to be insufficient. In Roman Law the *Interrogationes in iure* had occupied a distinct place during the period of the Formulary System. These *interrogationes* were the questions which the plaintiff asked of the defendant in order to determine the personal liability of the party in certain actions allowed in Roman Law. The defendant was under obligation to answer truthfully, otherwise he was to be held responsible in full for the claim. These two usages, the Germanic and the Roman, combined to form the use of the *positiones* in ecclesiastical procedure.[15]

The *positiones*, which are adequately rendered in English by the term allegations, were described as positive assertions of some fact, relative to the suit, to which the adverse party was obliged to answer. If the allegation was acknowledged as being true, then the one who had made the charge or claim was relieved of the burden of proof for his statement. The defendant was obliged to answer to the allegation personally; if his advocate presumed to do so, the judge was empowered to expel him from the court.[16]

It suffices here to have made mention of the *positiones* or allegations and to have indicated what they implied. A fuller treatment will be accorded them in the next chapter, when the doctrine of the decretalists will be considered, for it is there

---

[13]*Speculum Iuris* (3 vols., Venetiis, 1577), Lib. II, Part. II, n. 1.

[14]Wanenmacher, *Canonical Evidence in Marriage Cases*, p. 62, n. 113.

[15]Engelmann-Millar, *History of Continental Civil Procedure* (Boston: Little Brown and Co., 1927; Vol. VII of *The Continental Legal Series*, 10 vols.), p. 472.

[16]Glossa s. v. *positiones*, ad c. 1, *de confessis*, II, 9, in VI°.

that the commentary on this new mode of procedure properly belongs.

iii. The Contumacious Refusal to Answer

In order to ensure the effectiveness of the interrogation as a means of investigating the truth, it was considered necessary even with the earliest developments of judicial procedure to penalize one who contumaciously refused to answer the legitimate judicial interrogations. It can easily be seen that, if the party could with impunity disregard these judicial inquiries after the truth, they would be of no practical value at all and soon would fall into desuetude. For, if such an option had been granted, then the party could have returned an answer simply when he considered that his reply would be favorable to himself.

In Roman Law the contumacious refusal to answer was construed as a confession relative to the point in question. In Ecclesiastical Law this was also true. But, as both Ivo and Burchard[17] pointed out, ecclesiastical penalties up to and including excommunication, could be imposed not only upon those who refused to answer but also upon those who refused to appear in court. However, those who possessed benefices could not be deprived of these except by means of a judicial sentence which abstracted from the factor of confession as furnishing any proof or evidence.

iv. Torture

In proportion to the rising importance of the judicial factor of confession, torture as a mode of examination comes to the fore. In the secular law systems, both Roman and Germanic, torture and ordeals played an important part. The important rôle which torture played in Roman Law judicial proceedings was emphasized by Esmein to the point that he attributed the diffusion of torture in the court procedure of the Middle Ages to the revival of the half-forgotten Roman Law as occasioned by the criminalists of the School of

---

[17] Ivo, *Decretum*, V—MPL, CLXI, 297; Burchard, *Liber Decretorum*, 1 —*MPL*, CXL, 181.

Bologna.[18] Yet, though it is true that the employing of torture was considered as legitimate and useful in the secular courts, it is no less true that from the very beginning the Church repeatedly and categorically forbade its use in the ecclesiastical courts.[19] According to the pseudo-Isidorian decretal, Pope Alexander I (105-115) considered that any document extracted from persons through force, fear or fraud, or drawn up by them for the sake of gaining freedom from the duress, was without juridical effect and could not be introduced into ecclesiastical courts.[20]

Later documents of the Church condemned the use of torture and ordeals as unjust.[21] It was argued that proof of the commission of the crime was either at hand or it was lacking. If it was established by proof that the crime had been committed, then the penalties of law were to be enforced. On the other hand, if the commission of the crime could not be thus established, then torture was not to be used as a means of extracting a confession. For it was an offense against the natural law to torture an innocent person. But a person was to be regarded as innocent as long as the commission of a crime by him was not duly established through proof and evidence.

The authors also argued that, if torture could be applied indiscriminately with a view to exacting a confession, then more often than not a person, in order to escape the pains of the torture to which he would be subjected if he did not admit that he perpetrated the crime, would confess to a crime

---

[18]Esmein-Simpson, *A History of Continental Criminal Procedure*, p. 9.

[19]Król, *The Defendant in Ecclesisatical Trials*, The Catholic University of America Canon Law Studies, n. 146, (Washington, D.C.: The Catholic University of America Press, 1942), p. 24.

[20]"Similiter si huiusmodi personis quaedam scripturae quoquo modo per vim, per metum aut fraudem extortae fuerint, vel ut se liberare possint, quocumque ab eis conscriptae vel roboratae fuerint ingenio, ad nullum eis praeiudicium aut nocumentum pervenire censemus."—Mansi, *Sacrorum Conciliorum Nova et Amplissima Collectio* (53 vols. in 60, Paris, Arnhem, Leipzig, 1901-1927), I, 637, 2; cf. also Hinschius, *Decretales Psuedo-Isidorianae et Capitula Angrilrammi*, p. 97.

[21]Nicholaus I, *Epist. ad Carolum Calvum—MPL*, CXIX, 1144; c. 20, c. II, q. 5; Agobard, *Liber Adversus legem Grundobaldi; Liber contra Judicium Dei—MPL*, CIV, 125, 254.

of which he was not guilty.[22] Thus it was considered the duty of earthly rulers to pass judgment on only those crimes for which proof was established either through the spontaneous confession of the party or through convincing testimony furnished by witnesses. The occult and the unknown were to be left to God, Who alone knows the secrets of the hearts of men.

In so far, then, as the rule for ecclesiastical courts was concerned, torture was either not used at all, or used only on rare occasions, namely, when light coercive punishment was invoked in retribution for a party's contumacious attitude. In the realm of fact, however, there were abuses which pointed to the use of torture and of the trial by ordeal as actual occurrences.

---

[22]Vecchiotti, *Institutiones Canonicae* (16 ed., 3 vols., Augustae Taurinorum, 1875), II, 304.

CHAPTER III

THE JUDICIAL INTERROGATION OF THE PARTIES FROM THE TIME OF GRATIAN TO THE COUNCIL OF TRENT

Article 1. The Decretals

Ecclesiastical judgments, as found in the schema of the Decretal Collections, form, for the most part, the subject matter of the second of the five books. There one finds a wealth of legislation on the procedural norms then current. At the time, these norms were not arranged systematically according to the successive order in a judicial procedure. However, when properly arranged, they afford a rather complete picture of the *ordo iudiciarius* as it existed during that period of procedural development.[1]

. Actually there appears very little legislation regarding the interrogations of the parties. In great part this was probably due to the fact that Roman Law legislation on this phase of judicial procedure was considered as adequate.[2] This assumption seems verified in the fact that most of the glosses which made reference to this matter offered merely a summary of the pertinent passages of Roman Law. But the extant legislation, as supplemented by the glosses of the older Decretal Collections, enables one to form a clear concept of the interrogatory part of the trial.

The glosses were added to the Decretal Collections by a group of men nowadays referred to as the glossators. Their additions consisted of marginal notes, which had for their purpose the offering of a fuller explanation, the tracing of

---

[1]Wernz, *Ius Decretalium* (2. ed., 6 vols., Rome et Prati, 1906-1913), V, p. 8, n. 11.

[2]Cocchi, *Commentarium in Codicem Iuris Canonici* (8 vols. in 5, Vol. VII, 4. ed., Augustae: Marietti, 1940), VII, 223.

sources, the deduction of certain conclusions, and the proposing of contrary or parallel texts.[3]

Article 2. The Judicial Interrogation of the Parties

i. The Right to Interrogate.

In a number of passages found in the Gloss of the Decretals, there is reiterated the Roman Law principle that the judge has the right and duty to interrogate the parties as often as he believes it necessary, that is, whenever, as Roman Law has it, he is moved by a sense of equity to seek more information in order to arrive at the truth of the matter to be adjudicated.[4]

As in Roman Law, so in the Decretal Law, not only the judge but also the parties and their advocates were permitted to interrogate each other. However, the interrogations addressed by the parties to each other differed from those addressed by the judge to them.[5] For, before it was possible for one party to question the other, it was necessary for him to take an oath not to interrogate with an evil intent. It was otherwise with the judge, for he, in virtue of his high office and in consequence of the incumbent obligation of rendering a just decision, was permitted, without such a preliminary, to interrogate the parties at the trial.

ii. Oaths in Ecclesiastical Trials.

Three oaths played an important part in the ecclesiastical trials of the time, and had an especial bearing on the interrogations of the parties.

The first of these oaths was the *iuramentum calumniae*

---

[3]Van Hove, *Commentarium Lovaniense in Codicem Iuris Canonici*, Vol. I, Tom. I, *Prolegomena ad Codicem Iuris Canonici* (2. ed., Mechliniae et Romae: H. Dessain, 1945), p. 426.

[4]Glossa s. v. *interrogandi*, ad c. 11, C. XXX, q. 5; glossa s. v. *de confessis*, ad c. 3, X, *de confessis*, II, 18; glossa s. v. *interrogationibus*, ad c. 6, X, *de iuramento calumniae*, II, 17; glossa s. v. *interrogationes*, ad c. 11, X, *de probationibus*, II, 19; glossa 1, ad c. 1, *de confessis*, II, 9, in VI°; c. 2, *de verborum singnificatione*, V, 11, in Clem.

[5]Glossa s. v. *interrogandi*, ad c. 11, C. XXX, q. 5.

vitandae, the oath to avoid calumny.[6] Today, mention of this oath has all but been suppressed in the Code of law. It receives mention but once in the present legislation, in canon 2037, §4, which imposes the taking of this oath upon the postulators and the vice-postulators in causes of beatification.

The Law of the Decretals borrowed this oath from Roman Law, and made it a *sine qua non* condition for all contentious cases by requiring it of the plaintiff as well as of the defendant. It was, as it had been under Justinian, the chief means of avoiding vexatious litigation.

Five points were contained in the oath to avoid calumny: 1) the litigant swore to his belief in the justice of his cause; 2) he swore that when interrogated he would not deny that which he believed to be the truth; 3) he swore that he would not knowingly employ false proofs; 4) he swore that he would not seek a fraudulent delay in the trial; and lastly, 5) he swore that he had not given, and that he would not give or promise anything, save to those persons with reference to whom the law permitted him so to do.[7]

The plaintiff who refused to take this oath lost his right of action as a dishonest litigant. On the other hand, the refusal of this oath by the defendant was considered as an admission of the charges as set forth by the plaintiff.[8]

The *iuramentum malitiae* in Decretal Law was closely akin to the oath to avoid calumny. This oath has, however, been left completely unmentioned in the present Code. It was employed, not to establish the truth of the whole trial as such, but to establish the truth in certain points of the trial. It could be demanded whenever in the opinion of the judge there arose a suspicion that one of the litigants had a malicious intent in view.[9]

The oath to avoid calumny was usually taken at the be-

---

[6]C. (2, 58) (1, 9); c. 2, X, *de iuramento calumniae,* II, 7; Moriarty, *Oaths in Ecclesiastical Courts,* The Catholic University of America Canon Law Studies, n. 110 (Washington, D. C.: The Catholic University of America Press, 1937), p. 3.

[7]Glossa ad c. 1, X, *de iuramento calumniae,* II, 7.

[8]C. 7, X, *de iuramento calumniae,* II, 7.

[9]C. 2, *de iuramento calumniae,* II, 4 in VI°.

ginning of the trial, immediately after the joining of issue. The *iuramentum malitiae*, on the other hand, could be tendered either before or after the joining of issue, and in any part of the trial.[10] It was this latter oath, the *iuramentum malitiae*, which the party who was about to question had to take in order to signify to the court that his motives in interrogating the other party were above suspicion.

The remaining oath was the *iuramentum de veritate dicenda*. It, too, played an important part in the judicial processes of the time. It was a promissary oath by which the taker bound himself to tell the truth and nothing but the truth. Boniface VIII (1294-1303) recommended the use of this oath along with the *iuramentum calumniae vitandae* in all ecclesiastical trials, but indicated simultaneously that the unintentional omission of these two oaths did not render the process null.[11]

The *iuramentum de veritate dicenda* had its origin in both the Roman and Germanic Law Systems. In Roman Law the *iusiurandum calumniae* corresponded to the *iuramentum de veritate dicenda* of the parties, as it is found in the present canonical procedure. In Roman Law, however, the *iuramentum de veritate dicenda* was imposed only upon the witnesses before they testified; it had no reference to the parties.[12]

At exactly what period of canonical procedure it became customary to demand of the parties the *iuramentum de veritate dicenda* instead of the *iuramentum calumniae vitandae*, or, as it is sometimes called, the *iusiurandum calumniae*, is impossible to determine. Undoubtedly a certain decretal of Honorius II (1124-1130) had some influence in effecting this change. This pontiff ordained that in the *causae spirituales* the oath to avoid calumny was to be foregone, for, he remarked, such trials were to be judged on the principles of canonical equity, and not on the strict principles of law.

---

[10] Reiffenstuel, *Ius Canonicum Universum* (5 vols. in 7, Parisiis, 1864-1870), Lib. II, Tit. 24, 1, n. 3.

[11] C. 1, *de iuramento calumniae*, II, 4, in VI°.

[12] C. (4, 20) 9.

The *Glossa* to this passage stated that in such cases it was customary to demand of the parties the *iuramentum de veritate dicenda.*[13] Later, as has already been pointed out, Boniface VIII advised the use of both of these oaths in all trials, including the *causae spirituales.*[14]

iii. The Time for the Interrogations

The judge could interrogate whenever he felt that more information was necessary in order to arrive at a just and equitable solution of the matter in question. The exercise of his right, in so far as the element of time was concerned, was limited only by the final judicial sentence,[15] so that both before and after the joining of issue, and even after the conclusion of the case itself, but before the final judicial sentence, the judicial interrogation could be carried out.[16] However, the judge was advised that he should attempt to make all necessary interrogations before the conclusion of the case.[17]

In 1306, desiring to clarify the wording of the papal commissions to the judges, Clement V (1305-1314) issued his constitution, *Saepe,* in which he provided for a simplified system of procedure.[18] It was in reality the forerunner of the summary procedure of today. In this constitution it was stated that in certain cases, namely in those concerned with benefices, marriage and usury, the judge could proceed without following the solemn procedural form.[19] The use of this form was no longer mandatory. It was desired that ecclesiastical judgments might be speeded up. But even with reference to these cases the judge was explicitly advised that he had the right and the duty to interrogate the parties either at their insistence or *ex officio,* as often as equity demanded it.

---

[13]Glossa ad c. 2, X, *de iuramento calumniae,* II, 7.

[14]C. 1, *de iuramento calumniae,* II, 4 in VI°; cf. Moriarty, *Oaths in Ecclesiastical Courts,* p. 28.

[15]C. 10, X, *de fide instrumentorum,* II, 22.

[16]Glossa ad c. 3, X, *de confessis,* II, 18; glossa ad c. 6, X, *de iuramento calumniae,* II, 7; glossa ad c. 1, X, *de litis Contestatione,* II, 5.

[17]C. 5, X, *de causa possessionis et proprietatis,* II, 12.

[18]C. 2, *de verborum significatione,* V, 11, in Clem.

[19]C. 2, *de iudiciis,* II, 1, in Clem.

In certain cases, particularly in those concerned with real rights, the judge was obliged to interrogate the parties before the joining of issue. If he omitted to do so, the entire proceedings were to be considered as null.[20] The judge was required to ask whether the defendant had in his possession the property in question. If he had possession, then did he still possess it in its entirety or only in part? And if the defendant disclaimed possession, he was to be asked in what manner he dispossessed himself, rightfully or fraudulently. It was also stated that if the plaintiff established that the defendant mendaciously denied his possession of the property, then the judge was to give the property to the plaintiff, even though the claims of the latter to the property had not as yet been substantiated.

A similarity may be noted between the *"Interrogationes in iure"* of the Roman Law and the questions which the judge was to propose before the joining of issue. However, in Roman Law it was the party himself who proposed the questions. The judge thereupon was to take cognizance of the answers in drawing up the formula for the joining of issue.

iv. The Joining of Issue *(Litis Contestatio)*

Since the joining of issue had been mentioned several times in the preceding articles, it is important that a few words be said about this important phase of the trial. The joining of issue was the beginning and the foundation for the entire trial. Without it the subsequent proceedings were considered to be null.[21].

After the citation of the defendant, the plaintiff asserted his claims in the presence of the judge and the other party. The defendant then had the choice of confessing to the claims of the plaintiff or of contradicting them. If he confessed, then there was in reality no joining of issue, unless the confession was qualified.[22] The confession became qualified when-

---

[20]Glossa s. v. *interrogationibus et responsionibus*, ad c. 6, X, *de iuramento calumniae*, II, 7.

[21]Glossa s. v. *responsiones*, ad c. 1, X, *de litis contestatione*, II, 5.

[22]Wernz, *Ius Decretalium*, V. 362; Reiffenstuel, *Ius Canonicum Universum*, Lib. II, tit. 5, n. 20.

ever the defendant attempted to justify his actions. But if, instead of confessing, the accused contradicted the claims of the plaintiff, then there resulted the joining of issue.[23] For this reason the defendant was to be interrogated prior to the interrogations of the witnesses. If a confession was made by the defendant, then there was no need of a trial or of the calling of witnesses. Likewise the accused was thus afforded an opportunity for advancing any justifying motives in warrant of his act.[24]

There seems to have been some confusion as to who actually proposed the claims of the plaintiff to the defendant. Whether it was the judge at the request of the plaintiff, or simply the plaintiff himself, is not quite clear. From the generality of the texts it seems that it was the judge who conducted the interrogation, but that the joining of issue was nevertheless validly effected if the plaintiff had interrogated in the presence of the judge.[25]

The basis for contending that the plaintiff himself could make the interrogation was contained in the Roman Law. For there it was considered as a principle of law that the questioning of one party by the other was the equivalent of a judicial interrogation.[26] In any case it was necessary for the defendant to manifest his intention of contesting the claims of the plaintiff if there was to be a valid joining of issue. The mere fact that certain questions were asked of the accused was not sufficient.[27] Thus, for a valid joining of issue four things were required, namely, the petition of the plaintiff, the contradiction of the defendant, the presence of the judge, and the intention of the parties to contest the claims.

---

[23]"Litis contestatio fieri debet interrogante iudice, actore proponente suam actionem, et reo respondente ad interrogantem iudicem" —glossa ad c. 1, X, *de litis contestatione*, II, 5.

[24]Glossa s. v. *additio*, ad c. 24, X, *de accusationibus, inquisitionibus et denunciationibus*, V, 1.

[25]". . . . . . . .perinde est ac si a iudice interrogaretur, et per talem interrogationem et responsionem fit litis contestatio, ut dicitur in fine; nec distinguitur per quem fiat interrogatio."—glossa s. v. *instante actore*, ad c. 4, X, *de dolo et contumacia II*, 4.

[26]D. (40, 1) (11, 5)—this Roman Law principle is quoted in the just cited gloss.

[27]C. 10, X, *de probationibus*, II, 19.

The information obtained from the defendant prior to the joining of issue could not be used for the defendant's condemnation, unless it was again introduced into the case by the plaintiff after the joining of issue. Thus, apart from an effected *litis contestatio* and the subsequent petition of the plaintiff, the earlier interrogations were of no judical value as far as the solution of the case was concerned.[28]

v. The Use of Torture

It had indeed been claimed that the use of torture was introduced into the ecclesiastical courts either on the order of Alexander III (1159-1181) or during his pontificate.[29] But the specified procedure in the ecclesiastical tribunals leads in reality to the opposite conclusion. As for the aforementioned decree of Alexander III, it should be pointed out that the coercion, as there contemplated, was to be applied only to a thief who already had been convicted and who, nevertheless, steadfastly refused to return his loot to its rightful owner. The torture, therefore, served as a means of forcing the thief to return stolen property, rather than as a method of making him confess to a crime as yet unproved.[30]

The IV General Council of the Lateran (1215) forbade any priestly approbation or blessing to be conferred upon those who subjected themselves to the ordeal by the hot or cold water or by the hot iron.[31]

Thus the Church continuously proscribed the use of torture and of ordeals. If nevertheless they were put to use in the ecclesiastical courts on occasion, that fact reflected the outcropping of abuses rather than the accepted form of procedure.[32]

[28]Glossa s. v. *responsiones*, ad c. 1, X, *de litis contestatione*, II, 5.

[29]C. 1, X, *de deposito*, III, 16.

[30]Vecchiotti, *Institutiones Canonicae*, II, 306.

[31]C. 18—Mansi, XXII, 1007. This canon was incorporated in the *Corpus Iuris Canonici* as c. 9, X, *ne clerici vel monachi saecularibus negotiis se immisceant*, III, 50.

[32]Bouix, *Tractatus de Judiciis Ecclesiasticis* (2 vols. in 1, Parisiis, 1855), II, 364 (hereafter cited *De Judiciis Ecclesiasticis*); Droste- Messmer, *Canonical Procedure in the Disciplinary and Criminal Cases of Clerics*, p. 19; Von Bar, *A History of Continental Criminal Law* (translated by Thomas S. Bell, Boston: Little, Brown & Co., 1916; Vol. IV of *The Continental Legal Series*, 10 vols.), p. 180.

Article 3. The *Positiones*

Upon the joining of issue and the taking of the oath to avoid calumny, there followed the making of the allegations *(positiones)*. As has already been pointed out in the preceding chapter on the canonical procedure which obtained before the time of Gratian, the parties' use of the allegations in a trial is thought to have had its rise at some time during that period. The exact time of the beginning of their use is not known, but it is evident that during the era of the decretalists the use of such allegations in court procedure existed as an already accepted institution.[33] It should again be recalled that this juridical institute derived its existence in part from both the Roman and the Germanic procedural practices.[34]

The *positiones* were positive assertions of facts invested with a substantial import for the suit of the plaintiff. To these assertions the adverse party was obliged to answer. His answer had to be in support of the assertion if the one who made the allegation was to stand relieved of the burden of proof.[35] Both parties could make use of the allegations during the course of the trial.[36] But it seems that one and the same allegation as made by one of the parties could not in identical fashion be returned by the other party.[37] In general, of course, it was the plaintiff who submitted the allegation for an answer from his adversary in the trial.

For the drawing up of the allegations, the claims of the plaintiff, as formulated in the bill of complaint presented at the joining of issue, were subdivided into distinct points or counts. These were then embodied in a form of positive statements, that is, of statements that called for a simple answer of "yes" or "no" as manifesting agreement or disagreement on the side of the adverse party. Thus, for instance, the chal-

---

[33]Glossa s. v. *longaevus*, ad c. 2, *de verborum significatione*, V. 11, in Clem.; Durantis, *Speculum Iuris*, II, 583.

[34]Engelmann-Millar, *A History of Continental Civil Procedure*, p. 472.

[35]C. 10, X, *de probationibus*, II, 9; glossa s. v. *statuimus*, ad c. 1, *de confessis*, II, 9, in VI°.

[36]Vecchiotti, *Institutiones Canonicae*, II, 292.

[37]Hostiensis, *Summa Aurea* (Lugduni, 1568), Lib. II, Tit. *De Iudiciis*, n. 8.

lenging statement would be worded: ''You admit that you are
the heir in question.'' If the party to whom such a statement
was addressed admitted that he was the heir, then the party
who originated the statement was relieved of any further obligation of proving the contention implied in it. On the other
hand, if the statement was denied by the challenged party,
then conclusive proof had to be introduced if the stated fact
was to prove acceptable to the court. Thus the purpose of the
invoked allegations was to speed up the judicial process by
determining at the outset of the trial just what assertion or
claim still called for conclusive proof. In this way there was
forestalled much vexatious litigation with regard to points that
were readily admitted to be true.[38].

Since an allegation which was admitted to be true by the
adverse party satisfied all need of proof, it had to be proposed
after the joining of issue and before the conclusion of the
case, if it was to have any juridical value as proof in the
settlement of the cause.[39]

The party who submitted the allegation was obliged to
take an oath, the *iuramentum malitiae,* in order to satisfy the
court of his good faith.[40] The one who was confronted with
the allegation likewise was required to take an oath, the
iuramentum de veritate dicenda, whereby he bound himself
to tell the truth.[41]

Claims and statements of a negative character, that is,
those for which proof according to the strict letter of the
law was available only through the confession of the party,
could not be invoked as allegations in the trial. Only such
matters which lent themselves for possible proof in the external
forum could be invoked as points or counts in the allegation.
Nevertheless, Innocent IV (1243-1245) allowed the use of
negative claims and statements as allegations if in equity the
judge considered it proper to permit them to be invoked.[42]

---

[38]C. 2, *de verborum significatione*, V. 11, in Clem.
[39]Glossa s. v. *statuimus*, ad. c. 2, *de confessis*, II, 9, in VI°.
[40]Vecchiotti, *Institutiones Canonicae*, II, 292.
[41]C. 2, *de testibus et attestationibus*, II, 10, in VI°.
[42]C. 1, *de confessis*, II, 9, in VI°.

It was the duty of the judge to examine the proposed allegations and to pass upon their admissability. He was empowered by means of an interlocutory decree to reject those which he found to be ambiguous and deceptive, or which were impertinent to the case. To afford the judge an opportunity of examining these beforehand, it was necessary that they be submitted to him in writing.[43] If use was made of an allegation which contained several parts, one of which was true but the other was false, the adverse party was permitted to deny the entire assertion as false, since any allegation which in its import remained indefinite and uncertain was to be regarded as nugatory in its effect.[44]

It seems that in the beginning the *positiones* were also called *articuli,* and that at least in the early Decretal Law these two terms were used indiscriminately.[45] However, as in the course of time legal concepts became defined more clearly, it seems that the term *articulus* became accepted as referring to only a *positio* which the adverse party denied to be true, and which consequently could be substantiated only by means of conclusive proof.[46]

Lastly, the use of the allegations was allowed only in civil cases, that is, in those which according to the present law are designated as contentious cases.[47] In criminal causes the judge had to resort to interrogations in the place of the party's allegations as the means wherewith to obtain equal proof.[48]

Article 4. The Interrogations and the *Positiones*

The contrast between a party's allegations and the judge's interrogations reflects many distinctions. Nevertheless, the use

---

[43]Glossa s. v. *statuimus,* ad c. 1, *de confessis,* II, 9, in VI°; Hostiensis, *Summa Aurea,* Lib. II, tit. 117, n. 8.

[44]Glossa s. v. *sigillatim,* ad c. 2, *de testibus et attestationibus,* II, 10, in VI°.

[45]"........actor deducit suum factum quod continetur in libello per articulos; et illi articuli vocantur positiones."—glossa s. v. *statuimus,* ad c. 1, *de confessis,* II, 9, in VI°.

[46]Smith, *Elements of Ecclesiastical Law* (3 vols., Vol. II, *Ecclesiastical Trials,* 5. ed., New York: Benziger Bros., 1887), II, 221.

[47]Canon 1552 § 2, n. 1.

[48]Reiffenstuel, *Ius Canonicum Universum,* Lib. II, Tit. 18, n. 21.

of allegations as regulated by the procedural laws counted as a species of judicial interrogation. Thus the consideration of allegations has a very definite place in the historical study of the judicial interrogation of the parties. Durantis claimed that the distinction between allegations and interrogations was one which evinced not an essential but simply a modal difference.[49]

In the first place, the primary purpose of the interrogations was the obtaining of information that led to the truth of the case. For this reason the interrogations took the form of questions. The allegations took the form of positive assertions, which in the challenge that they implied called either for an admission or for a denial on the part of the adverse party, so that in the event of a confession the trial might become considerably shortened.

The interrogations ordinarily were to be made by the judge, although it was permissible under the Decretal Law for the parties to question each other. But the allegations were usually made by the party himself under the surveillance of the judge.

The advocate as well as the party could respond to the judicial interrogation, but to the allegations only the party could reply. If the advocate nevertheless presumed to answer, his response was of no juridical efficacy, and the judge could also expel him from the court.[50]

Finally, the interrogations could be employed in both contentious and criminal trials, whereas the use of the allegations was restricted to contentious causes, since in all criminal causes the defendant was regarded as innocent until the contrary was established by means of strict proof. To have had any value in a criminal cause, the allegation would have had to postulate the defendant's readiness to confess his guilt, which as an assumption was hardly ever supported in fact.

Vecchiotti (+1870) indeed stated that the use of the allegations did at times appear in criminal trials, but he likewise

---

[49]*Speculum Iuris*, Lib. II, Part. II, n. 1.
[50]Glossa s. v. *statuimus*, ad c. 1, *de confessis*, II, 9, in VI°.

maintained that the defendant was never subjected to the taking of an oath, and that his refusal to answer or to appear in court could never be considered as the equivalent of a confession. For in criminal causes, so he added, the proofs always had to be very clear and weighty before a sentence of condemnation was duly warranted.[51]

Article 5. The Obligation to Respond

As in Roman Law, so in the Decretal Law, the refusal to reply to the legitimate interrogations of the judge was considered as tantamount to a confession relative to the point at issue.[52]

But, it is to be noted that, if before the joining of issue the defendant refused to reply, or if he contumaciously refused to appear in court, his action was not the equivalent of a confession, but he was liable to ecclesiastical penalties for his act of contumacy.[53] The rule was not the same once the joining of issue had taken place and the oath to avoid calumny had been taken, for at that stage of the trial the refusal to answer was the equivalent of a confession. The glossators, however, made the distinction between the one who was simply interrogated and the one who in addition was ordered to reply. Accordingly, if a party was simply interrogated and thereupon withdrew from the court before he was ordered to reply, it was not felt that his action implied a confession, but he was held liable to punishment for contumacy.[54]

A party was not obliged to reply to the interrogations of his adversary, unless he was ordered to do so by the court. Nevertheless, if a response was given, it was regarded as of equal effect with the response given to an interrogation duly made by the court.[55]

---

[51]Vecchiotti, *Institutiones Canonicae*, II, 292.

[52]C. 1, X, *de postulatione praelatorum*, I, 5; glossa s. v. *confessiones*, ad c. 11, X, *de probationibus*, II, 9.

[53]C. 1, X, *de iudiciis*, II, 1.

[54]Glossa ad c. 2, *de confessis*, II, 9, in VI°.

[55]Glossa 1, ad c. 6, X, *de iuramento calumniae*, II, 7.

With reference to the obligation of responding to the judicial interrogation, it was necessary to distinguish, as most of the authors did, between legitimate and non-legitimate interrogations. One's obligation of replying abated in the face of non-legitimate interrogations, and accordingly the court could not urge any obligation of responding under such circumstances. This distinction was one of paramount importance.

The legitimacy of the interrogations was in the main concerned with the observance by the judge of the judicial norms of procedure and with the matter of the interrogations themselves. In the first place, the judge had to possess judicial competence. In the period here under consideration, it seems that competence over a criminal cause was obtained either through the denunciation, or through the accusation, of the criminal before the court, or through the public infamy that was connected with the crime.[56] In civil or contentious causes the court became competent when the plaintiff presented his claims before it. But, whenever the judge lacked judicial competence, he had no right to interrogate or to demand that oaths be taken.

Secondly, in regard to the matter of the interrogation, a defendant was not to be interrogated concerning crimes that remained occult. For it was argued that the Church did not judge occult crimes for the reason that these were left to the judgment of God.[57]

Inasmuch as a previous accusation, denunciation or status of public infamy of the defendant was postulated for the validity of the trial, and consequently for the admissibility of the interrogations, it followed that judicial interrogations could not be made with regard to crimes other than those which were affected in the manner here indicated. A further reason for the mandatory omission of the interrogation re-

---

[56]Cc. 17, 19, 24, X, *de accusationibus, inquisitionibus et denunciationibus*, V, 1.

[57]Glossa s. v. *exceptis occultis criminibus*. ad c. 17, X, *de accusationibus, inquisitionibus et denunciationibus*, V, 1; glossa s. v. *secretorum*, ad c. 11, D. XXXII; glossa s. v. *si omnia*, ad c. 7, C. VI, q. 1.

lative to such crimes was the fact that the judicial order was best observed if the inquiry was not concerned with many things, but was restricted to the principal and immediate matter which formed the object of the process.[58]

What, then, were the means of redress which a defendant could employ if he was called on to reply to illegitimate interrogations? Since a refusal to answer could be construed as a confession, St. Thomas (1225-1274) maintained that the defendant could either appeal the illegality of the questions to a higher tribunal, or resort to subterfuge or ambiguity in his answer, short of course of lying.[59] St. Thomas added that if the accused, when legitimately interrogated, either refused to answer or answered with a lie, he sinned mortally, since he violated a serious obligation of justice, which at all times binds the subject to obey his lawful superiors in those things to which the superior's right extends.[60]

Any doubt as to the legitimacy of the interrogations was to be resolved in favor of the defendant, since it was a principle of law that in doubtful issues the favor and the protection of law yielded to the benefit of the defendant rather than to that of the plaintiff.[61]

Article 6. The Inquisition

A word must be said about the Inquisition of the Holy Office. To say the least, it is a subject which has caused much controversy. Catholics have perhaps been overzealous in attempting to defend this institution of the Middle Ages, whereas non-Catholics have striven to deny the very divinity of the Church because of it. As a result, exaggerations on both sides have beclouded the true nature of this process.

---

[58] Santi, *Praelectiones Iuris Canonici iuxta Ordinem Decretalium Gregorii IX* (2 vols., Ratisbonae, 1886), Lib. II, tit. 18, n. 15.

[59] "Si vero iudex hoc exquirat quod non potest secundum ordinem iuris, non tenetur ei accusatis respondere; sed potest vel per appellationem vel aliter licite subterfugere. Mendacium tamen dicere non licet."—St. Thomas, *Summa Theologica*, IIa, IIae, q. 69, art. 1.

[60] Cf. St. Thomas, *ibid.*, q. 67, art. 1.

[61] "Cum sunt partium iura obscura, reo favendum est potius quam actori."—Reg. 11, R. J., in VI°.

The Inquisition was an emergency tribunal instituted in the Middle Ages for the suppression of heresy. In the society of the time, when both Church and State were Christian, heresy was looked upon not only as a serious sin, but was regarded also as a most serious crime against the civil authorities. Thus it was that both the Church and State co-operated to root out an evil which was looked upon as dangerous to sound morals as well as to sound doctrine—for a corrupt tree brings forth corrupt fruit, and a man who believes falsely will act wrongly.[62]

With the spread of heresy throughout the Christian World, the Church and the State regarded themselves, when they saw the ordinary means of enforcement a failure, as justified in using more stringent means to suppress this danger to their very existence. In consequence of this endeavor, a special Inquisitor was appointed in each diocese to investigate anyone accused of heresy. These cases were tried, not according to the ordinary mode of procedure, but in a summary manner. In these trials it seems almost certain that torture was used.

But it was not used, as some writers would have us believe, according to the good pleasure of the tribunal without any regard for the evidence presented in the case. The general rule was that torture could not be used for the obtaining of a confession from the defendant, unless there had already been obtained against him at least semi-proof of his guilt.[63]

It is to be remembered, then, that the Inquisition of the Holy Office was an emergency institution set up to combat heresy, and that it was not governed by the ordinary procedural laws of the Church. Thus the fact that torture was used in these trials does not weaken the contention that in the ordinary ecclesiastical trials the use of torture was condemned by the Church from the very beginning. To deny, however, that there were any injustices in this inquisitorial pro-

---

[62]Tuberville, *The Spanish Inquisition* (London: Thornton Butterworth, Limited, 1932), p. 3.

[63]Bouix, *De Judiciis Ecclesiasticis*, II, 389; Tuberville, *ibid.*, p. 91.

cedure, or to affirm that this extraordinary institution never trespassed upon propriety, is not the purpose of this dissertation.

In conclusion, the following excerpt from an article entitled, "Ought Catholics to Defend the Inquisition," by Fr. Broderick, S. J., may serviceably be reproduced here.

> (It was) Pope Gregory IX under whom the Mediaeval Inquisition may be said to have started, not indeed as a permanent tribunal but as an emergency measure. The emergency certainly was great, as never perhaps in history did the Christian Faith stand in deadlier peril from so many powerful enemies, Islam, Judaism, and dark heresies by the dozens, survivals and revivals of ancient error, as in the 13th and 14th centuries. It is a mere justice to a great Pope to say that he had at least the strongest provocation for breaking with the age-old milder tradition of Christendom which deprecated the use of violence in the interests of religion.... But to say that Pope Gregory had much provocation from the heretics with fantastic names and still more fantastic tenets is not equivalent to saying he was justified or acted in the Church's best interests in appealing to the secular arm.[64]

---

[64]Broderick, "Ought Catholics to Defend the Inquisition?"—The Month (London, 1864—), CLXXVII (1941), 118 ff.

CHAPTER IV

THE JUDICIAL INTERROGATION OF THE PARTIES FROM THE COUNCIL OF TRENT TO THE CODIFICATION OF THE CODE OF CANON LAW

Article 1. The Council of Trent (1545-1563)

In dependence on the Decretal Collections of the *Corpus Iuris Canonici*, the glossators and the decretalists had indicated a definite set of rules, worked out with considerable minuteness, for the interrogation of the parties in the ecclesiastical courts. Though a certain development of the canonical method of procedure in other particulars still continued, there was only silence for many years on the part of the Church's lawgivers as regards the judicial interrogation of the parties.

The Council of Trent, giving its wholehearted attention to the extermination of the abuses which existed at the time, did not overlook the enacting of legislation against such abuses which had crept into the canonical method of procedure. These it undertook to reform by means of salutary decrees, especially by increasing and strengthening the judicial power of the bishops, and by eliminating a number of cumbersome solemnities connected with canonical trials.

However, with regard to the subject under consideration, the Council of Trent confined its decrees within a single chapter. It decreed that thenceforth matrimonial and criminal causes were not to be left to the judgment of a dean, of an archdeacon, or of other inferiors, but that they were reserved to the exclusive examination and sole jurisdiction of the bishop.[1] Thus the right to conduct the judicial interrogation of the parties in matrimonial and criminal causes became reserved to the bishop or his delegate, to the exclusion of all inferior judges.

----

[1] Conc. Trident. sess. XXIV, *de ref.*, c. 20.

Article 2. The Council of Rome (1725)

A far-reaching change in the use of oaths in ecclesiastical courts was effected in the Provincial Council of Rome, which was held in the year 1725 under the immediate presiding authority of Benedict XIII (1724-1730). This Council brought about the complete suppression of the practice of tendering the oath to the defendant in criminal trials. The Council decreed in part the following:

> It must not be judged reprehensible that, because of changing conditions of the times and for reasons of necessity and utility, human laws and customs sometimes vary....Because of this, we consider the practice in some secular and ecclesiastical courts of judges, in the process of examining the defendant in criminal trials, to demand of them the oath *de veritate dicenda* to be well-established, even though the said practice was never established by law. On the other hand, as daily experience shows, no advantage accrues to the prosecution from this practice, and nothing is proven against the defendant by this custom (as the defendants usually deny the crimes of which they are charged). So true is this, that not only does no necessity of demanding the oath exist; nay more, the sacred character of the oath demands and requires the prohibiting of the oath under these circumstances. Hence it is that we, having weighed both sides of the question carefully, and following as closely as possible the practice of the well-organized tribunals, command that all oaths tendered to the defendants in criminal trials be completely abolished and suppressed ....Nor do we wish an oath of this kind to be exacted of the defendants in the future (unless they are examined as witnesses in the trials of other individuals), by any judge or official under any pretext, cause or artifice; otherwise an examination thus conducted and all the oaths of the process shall be null and void and shall lack all binding force against the criminal.[2]

---

[2] Tit. XIII, Caput 2—Mansi, 34B, 1872. Cf. Moriarty, *Oaths in Ecclesiastical Courts*, p. 33.

Several facts must be noted concerning this law of the Council. While it was a local enactment and embraced only the Italian dioceses, it gained widespread recognition through the fact that it emanated from the very centre of Christendom itself. It was the definite forerunner of Canon 1744, which now clearly endows the principle of this particular law with a universal application.[3]

Another oath likewise lapsed from use in the ecclesiastical courts. It was the *iuramentum calumniae*. Its disappearance can be traced, not to any positive enactment forbidding it, but rather to a custom against the law. Schmalzgrueber (1663-1735) adverted to the non-use of this oath in his day, particularly in the courts of France and Belgium.[4] And Wernz (1842-1914), a pre-Code author, furnished various proofs for the reasonableness of this custom against the use of this oath as it had been demanded in the earlier law.[5]

Article 3. Decrees of the Roman Congregations

i. Condemned Propositions

In 1679, a decree of the Holy Office condemned a number of propositions, two of which had a bearing on the judicial interrogation of the parties. The one was worded thus:

> Si quis vel solus, vel coram aliis, sive interrogatus sive propria sponte, sive recreationis causa, sive quocunque alio fine iuret, se non fecisse aliquid, quod revera fecit, intelligendo intra se aliquid aliud, quod non fecit, vel aliam viam ab ea, in qua fecit, vel quodvis aliud additum verum, revera non mentitur nec est periurus.

The other was stated as follows:

> Causa iusta utendi his amphilologiis est, quoties id necessarium aut utile est ad salutem corporis, honorem, res

---

[3] Moriarty, *ibid.*, p. 34.

[4] Schmalzgrueber, *Ius Ecclesiasticum Universum* (5 vols. in 12, Romae, ex Typographia Rev. Cam. Apostolicae, 1843-1845), VIII.

[5] Wernz, *Ius Decretalium*, V, p. 478, n. 28.

familiares tuendas, vel ad quemlibet alium virtutis actum, ita ut veritatis occultatio censeatur tunc expediens et studiosa.[6]

Thus if the judge questioned under oath, the party was obliged in conscience to speak truthfully. He could not resort to prevarication, to perjury, or to a pure mental reservation. In this connection, however, Reiffenstuel (1642-1703) observed that if the defendant in a criminal trial was interrogated by a judge who did not observe the proper judicial procedure, he was not obliged to reply directly to the interrogation, but he could answer in an ambiguous manner in order to elude the question. Yet it was never licit for the defendant to offer a false statement or a lie, since that was intrinsically evil. However, the defendant's falsified statement did not involve him in mortal sin, except under such circumstances in which the same kind of false statement would have implied a mortal sin if it had been made outside a judicial forum.[7]

Reiffenstuel also stated that there was some doubt regarding the very existence of an interrogated defendant's obligation of admitting a crime to which there was attached the death penalty, or some other very serious punishment. There were many learned men, so he said, who contended that even in this case the defendant was obligated to admit the fact of his crime whenever he was lawfully interrogated by the judge. But along with others he upheld the opinion which claimed that the defendant could rightfully deny his guilt, that is, without contracting any moral culpability for his act of denial, as long as there was any reasonable hope of evading the penalty. The reason for this doctrine was the following. The judge's precept as implied in his act of interrogation, namely, that the fact of

---

[6]S. C. S. Off., decr. 4 mart. 1679, nn. 26, 27—*Codicis Iuris Canonici Fontes, cura Emi Petri Card. Gasparri editi* (9 vols., Romae (Postea Civate Vaticana): Typis Polyglottis Vaticanis, 1923-1939) (Vols. VII-IX, ed. cura et studio Emi Iustiniani Card. Seredi), n. 754 (hereafter cited *Fontes*); Denzinger-Bannwart-Umberg, *Enchiridion Symbolorum, Definitionem, et Declarationum de Rebus Fidei et Morum* (21.-23. ed., Friburgi Brisgoviae: Herder & Co., 1937), nn. 1176, 1177 (hereafter cited as *Enchiridrion Symbolorum*).

[7]Reiffenstuel, *Ius Canonicum Universum*, Lib. II, tit. 18, n. 155.

the crime be admitted, could be issued only in due accommodation to a man's natural instinct for self-preservation. But that demand, as inherent in the natural law, would not be respected if one were absolutely obliged to admit the fact of a crime not yet fully established by proof, when the result of such a confession was the death penalty or a near-equivalent punishment.[8]

ii. The Instruction *Cum moneat Glossa* (1840) of the Sacred Congregation of the Council.[9]

The nineteenth century ushered in a new era in the development of canonical procedure. Many Instructions and Decrees issuing from the Sacred Congregations served to establish new norms of procedure and to clarify those already existing, particularly in regard to the procedure to be followed in matrimonial causes. This action was taken on the part of the Holy See because, as Benedict XIV (1740-1758) in the preceding century had claimed in his Constitution *Dei miseratione*, the great sacrament of matrimony was being subjected to much sacrilegious abuse through the carelessness and the unscrupulousness of ecclesiastical tribunals in the handling of causes which involved the matrimonial bond.[10]

In order to remedy this abuse, Benedict XIV had clearly defined the office and the duties of the defender of the bond. He had made him a party to the trial. His presence was required as a necessary condition for the validity and the integrity of any part of the trial. He was, therefore, to be present also at the judicial examination of the parties.

As has been previously remarked, the history of the canonical development of the judicial interrogation of the parties was characterized by a decided lack of legislation. The principles derived from Roman Law had paved the way for the canonical practice, but it was not until the Sacred Congregation of the Council issued the well-known Instruction, *Cum moneat Glossa,*

---

[8]Reiffenstuel, *ibid.,* n. 166.

[9]*Fontes,* n. 4069.

[10]*Fontes,* n. 318.

in 1840, that the interrogation of the parties became part of the written law of the Church.

This important Instruction, the forerunner of many decrees and instructions on this subject, reiterated once more the precepts of the Council of Trent and the demands of Benedict XIV that the ordinary, to the exclusion of the inferior judges, was to try all marriage causes in the courts of first instance, and that the defender of the bond was to be present at the proceedings. The sanction for the failure to cite him was again declared to be the nullity of the acts of the cause. Furthermore, this Instruction described in detail the procedure to be observed in the judicial interrogation with particular reference to matrimonial causes.

First there was to be determined a day on which the plaintiff, that is, the party alleging the nullity of the marriage, was to appear in court. Before this date the defender of the bond was to draw up a list of questions, the interrogatory, upon which the party was to be examined. These questions were enclosed in a sealed envelope and then handed to the chancellor or the notary employed in the cause, with the understanding that they be opened by a decree of the judge in the actual session appointed for the examination of the party.

The specification of this interrogatory of the defender did not, however, infringe upon the Roman Law principle which permitted the judge personally to add his own questions to the interrogatory whenever equity appeared to demand it for the sake of arriving at the truth of the matter under consideration. Thus the Instruction stated that during the course of the examination the judge could *ex officio* add further questions if, from the nature of the responses already given, he felt that an answer to the added questions would serve to clarify either the existing declarations of the party or any new circumstances which had been brought to light as a result of the interrogatory prepared by the defender. This procedure, so the Instruction noted, was to be understood as normative with regard to all interrogatories used in canonical trials.

On the date determined in the citation the party appeared at court, and in the presence of the defender and of the notary the oath *de veritate dicenda* was then to be administered by the judge. The latter then opened the sealed interrogatory and proposed each of the questions to the party.

During the interrogatory the notary incorporated into the acts of the cause both the questions asked of and the answers given by the party. If, perchance, the judge made use of his prerogative to ask further questions *ex officio*, then such interrogations were specifically to be designated as the judge's own in the minutes of the proceedings.

If the examination could not be completed in one session, then the judge prorogued the session by designating some future date for its resumption. When the examination had been completed, the notary read the responses that had been given. This he was to do in a clear and intelligible voice. Thus the party was furnished the opportunity of correcting any of his replies. Then the judge administered an oath to the plaintiff. In this the latter declared the truth of his statements, and promised not to divulge either the interrogations or his responses before the publication of the process. Finally the party signed his statements, or, if he could not write, he affixed a mark in the sign of a cross. The judge, the defender and the notary also signed the minutes, and then they were inserted in the acts of the cause.

The party, either immediately after being examined or at least before the publication of the process, could propose points or counts upon which, in view of their reference to the case, he wished the other party to be interrogated. If the other party had already been questioned, then he was to be cited again and in the presence of the defender of the bond he had to reply to the points raised by the adverse party.

At the completion of the interrogation of the plaintiff the defendant was to be cited and questioned according to the procedure outlined above. The points raised by the plaintiff and any new interrogations which were based upon the already given testimony of the plaintiff were to be included in this interrogatory according to the prudent judgment of the defender.

Thus in this Instruction of the Sacred Congregation of the Council there was outlined the precise practice to be observed in the judicial interrogation of the parties with special reference to matrimonial causes. The following decrees of the Sacred Congregations in the main simply issued more specific determinations of these principles.

iii. Supplementary Decrees

In the year 1858 the Sacred Congregation of the Holy Office issued an Instruction with particular reference to the procedure to be followed in matrimonial causes involving impotency.[11] After stating that the oath *de veritate dicenda* was to be administered, the Instruction advised the notary that in the minutes of the session there should be a record of the date, of the place and of the hour of the examination, as well as mention of the name of the judge who presided. It was also stated that as a general rule the plaintiff should be examined not only first, but also separately from the defendant and the witnesses.

At this point in the Instruction there was indicated a rule which certainly left a way open to misinterpretation. According to this document the matter of the interrogations was to be left to the judgment, the prudence and the sagacity of the judge. In order to assist him in the task of drawing up a well suited interrogatory, the Holy Office then listed a set of questions which were thought serviceable and opportune in such cases. This ruling appeared to be in conflict with that of the previous Instruction of the Sacred Congregation of the Council in 1840, wherein it had been stated that the duty of drawing up the interrogatory belonged to the defender of the bond, although simultaneously the right of the judge to ask further questions *ex officio* was duly safeguarded.[12]

---

[11]*Fontes*, n. 946.
[12]*Fontes*, n. 4069.

Since the Instruction of the Holy Office gave no indication that by it the earlier Instruction of the Sacred Congregation of the Council was abrogated, and inasmuch as the subsequent legislation tended to confirm the right of the defender to draw up the interrogatory, it seems that the rule as invoked by the Holy Office in its Instruction was really to be interpreted as referring to the discretionary power of the judge. In the last analysis, then, the defender drew up the interrogatory, but it belonged to the judge to decide the propriety and opportuneness of the questions. To claim that the ruling invoked by the Holy Office pointed simply to an exceptional procedural form for causes involving impotency does not seem logical in view of the purpose and the office of the defender and also in the light of the later legislation.[13]

In the years of 1878 and 1883 the Sacred Congregation for the Propagation of the Faith issued instructions on the procedure to be followed in the United States in criminal causes concerning clerics.[14] Practically nothing was stated about the interrogation of the defendant. The Instructions concerned themselves primarily with the inquisition or the previous investigation that was to be carried on by the delegates of the bishop in their determining of whether there was any basis in fact for the accusation of the cleric.

In 1883 two further Instructions were issued, one by the Holy Office to the Bishops of the Orient,[15] and the other by the Sacred Congregation for the Propagation of the Faith.[16] Both Instructions treated the procedure to be followed in matrimonial causes. In content these Instructions were substantially the same, and in wording they were very similar. They restated many of the rules contained in the Instruction of 1840, and then added a few more detailed observations on

---

[13]Canon 1968; S. C. C., 20 aug. 1887—*Acta Sanctae Sedis* (41 vols., Romae, 1865-1908), XX (1887), 441, n. XIV (hereafter cited as *ASS*).

[14]S. C. de Prop. Fide, instr. 20 iun. 1878—*ASS*, XII (1879), 88; instr. a 1883—*ASS*, XXIV (1891), 365; *Fontes*, n. 4900.

[15]S. C. S. Off., instr. (ad Ep. Rituum Orient.), a. 1883—*Fontes*, n. 1076.

[16]S. C. de Prop. Fide, instr. a. 1883—*Fontes*, n. 4901.

the different steps to be observed in the judicial interrogation of the parties.

Before the administration of any oath, the judge was to instruct the parties, especially those who were uneducated, about the sanctity of an oath. The notary was advised that in the minutes of the session he was to record the name, the condition, the status, and the nationality of the party along with his mention of the type of the oath taken.

Previous to the interrogation the parties were required to give proof of their probity and credibility. The evidence for this was usually to be sought in the form of testimonial letters from their pastor or from some other trustworthy person.

The plaintiff was to be examined first. Specially emphasized in the interrogation were the factors whereby the court was to determine the exact nature of the allegation made by him in opposition to the validity of the marriage, of the grounds for his claim, and of the proofs that could be advanced in substantiation of that claim. The plaintiff was also to be questioned about all the attendant circumstances, particularly those of which he had personal knowledge. But it was also permissible for him to introduce in his depositions whatever indications of the truth he had gathered from all sources. Finally, there were to be noted in the minutes of the session the names of the witnesses whom the plaintiff desired to be called, as also the various points and counts upon which he desired the adverse party to be questioned.

In accordance with the nature of the cause brought to trial, the parties were to be requested to produce in court any documents they possessed with reference to their marriage. A restatement of these documents was to be joined with the acts of the cause. The notary was advised to make a note of the date on which they had been received, and of the name of the person who had deposited them.

The Instruction finally issued a warning to the court, and in particular to the defender of the bond, to guard against all likely fraud and collusion, especially if the depositions of the parties were in absolute agreement.

Article 4. Regulations of the Sacred Roman Rota

The Sacred Roman Rota owed its reorganization in the first decade of the present century to the Constitution *Sapienti Consilio* of Pope Pius X (1903-1914). This Constitution was issued under date of June 29, 1908.[17] In this Constitution there were contained certain general precepts relative to the judicial procedure to be followed in this Roman Tribunal. With these general norms as a basis, the Roman Rota proceeded to draw up a more detailed system of procedural rules,[18] which received the force of law through the approval given by the Roman Pontiff in 1910.[19]

These norms were of far-reaching importance. The Roman Tribunal of the Sacred Rota in the very centre of Christendom stands as a model of efficiency and thoroughness for the diocesan curias of the world. As a result, the practical importance of these regulations consisted in the wide legal influence which they exerted.

When the present Code of Canon Law was promulgated by Benedict XV (1914-1922) on the Feast of Pentecost, 1917, the constitution and the competency of the Sacred Roman Rota were re-affirmed. Many of its procedural norms became the source from which were borrowed the universal law of today. This is particularly true of those canons which refer to the judicial interrogation of the parties.[20]

Since these norms of the Sacred Roman Rota constituted the proximate source of the present-day legislation on the interrogation of the parties, and since in general they sum up in a precise and detailed manner the conclusions derived from the historical development of this phase of the trial, they are summarized here as they are found in the articles of the *Regulae Servandae* as issued in 1910.

---

[17]*Lex Propria S. R. Rotae et Signaturae Apostolicae*, 29 iun 1908—*Acta Apostolicae Sedis, Commentarium Officiale* (Romae, 1909—), I (1909), 20-35 (hereafter cited *AAS*).

[18]Bernardini, "*Normae S. R. Rotae*"—*Apollinaris* (Romae, 1928—), VII (1934), 429-478.

[19]*Regulae Servandae in Iudiciis apud S. R. Rotae Tribunal*, 4 aug. 1910—*AAS*, II (1910), 783-850.

[20]Canons 1742-1746.

Art. 109, n. 1. In criminal trials, the persons who are accused of a crime are not to be placed under oath during the interrogation.

N. 2. In the event that the defendant lacks legal assistance the judge is to assign an advocate for him, for it is presumed that the accused is incapable of successfully conducting his own defense. The advocate may even assist at the interrogation.

Art. 110. If the parties and witnesses to be interrogated and examined cannot be present in the Roman Curia, their examination is to be delegated to judges to whom rogatory letters, to this effect, are to be sent.

Art. 137, n. 1. Both parties have the right to draw out of the judicial confession of the adverse party a proof of the facts pertinent to the cause.

N. 2. It is permitted even in criminal causes, and generally in all other causes which have reference to the public good, that the promoter of justice propose interrogations and allegations upon which the defendant is to be examined.

N. 3. In causes which are concerned with the matrimonial bond and the validity of sacred ordination, the defender of the bond enjoys the same privilege.

Art. 138. During the examination each party has the right to request that certain interrogations be made and allegations presented with a view to obtaining a confession from the adverse party. But the request must specify the individual counts regarding which an answer is sought from the adverse party.

Art. 139. When such a request is accepted by the court, it is the judge who orders the party to reply to the question, or to affirm or deny the presented allegation. If the party flaunts the precept of the judge, then the alleged facts will be deemed as true, and as admitted and confessed by the party.

Art. 140, n. 1. The judge shall not accept such a request from the party unless the interrogation or the allegation has reference to an important fact which is pertinent to the cause. He may also correct it, and in its place substitute another, which he considers to be more opportune.

N. 2. The allegation differs in form from the interrogation. For an allegation is an assertion of some fact which is proposed to the adverse party with the frank purpose that the latter will affirm or deny its truth.

Art. 141. The decree by means of which the allegations and the interrogations are accepted by the court must contain along with the text of the proposed questions and assertions the warning and the threat that, if the party refuses to answer or offers no reasonable excuse for his silence or his absence, the alleged facts will be regarded as true and substantiated by the party's confession.

Art. 142. In non-criminal causes the response of the party must be confirmed under oath.

Art. 144. Present at the giving of the reply must be the notary who makes a record in writing of the response. These he is to read to the party at the conclusion of the examination, in order that the latter be given an opportunity to correct or to make an addition to any of his replies, in the same way as this is done for the witnesses.

In conclusion, it may be stated that these norms of the Sacred Roman Rota do not differ substantially from the subsequent regulations issued in 1934.[21]

------

[21]*Normae S. R. Rotae Tribunalis*, 29 iun. 1934—*AAS*, XXVI (1934), 449-491.

PART II

CANONICAL COMMENTARY

CHAPTER V

INTRODUCTORY REMARKS ON THE JUDICIAL INTERROGATION OF THE PARTIES

Article 1. The Purpose of the Judicial Interrogation

Before a judge is permitted to pass sentence in a judicial trial, he must, from the acts and proofs gathered during the course of the judicial proceedings, have acquired moral certitude concerning the matter which he is called upon to adjudicate. In fact, if this moral certitude cannot be had regarding the justice and truth of the plaintiff's cause, he must dismiss the controversy as being of insufficient proof.[1]

As a means of acquiring this moral certitude, there are had in ecclesiastical law a number of procedural norms which constitute what is usually referred to as the probatory stage of a canonical trial. At the very outset of this probatory period, following the chronological order of a trial as outlined in the present law of the Code, there is had the judicial interrogation of the parties. This interrogation of the parties, however, is not limited to being merely a preliminary to the probatory period, but, as the Code itself points out, it may be resorted to by the judiciary up to and in some instances even after the actual conclusion of the period for the taking of evidence in the trial has been decreed by the judge.[2]

While it is of the nature of the *libellus* and of the *litis contestatio* to set down and to determine the specific point or points at issue, as well as to indicate in a general way at least the main

---

[1]Canon 1869.
[2]Canon 1742, § 3.

sources of proof, it cannot be said that they have brought to the attention of the tribunal all the facts and circumstances relative to a just solution of the cause.[3] To do this, that is, to permit the judge to become more fully informed regarding the object of the trial and the attendant facts and circumstances, the Code provides for the judicial interrogation of the parties.[4]

The judicial interrogation serves also to provide the judge with an opportunity to form some idea of the number, nature and availability of the proofs which the parties can and ought to produce, according to the nature and circumstances of the cause, to support and verify their respective claims. It is to be remembered that the parties themselves are vitally interested in the ultimate decision of the court. Thus their depositions, as their judicial responses are termed in order to distinguish them from the responses of the witnesses which are properly termed testimony, must most certainly be evaluated and verified if the whole truth and nothing but the truth is to be known.

It is obvious that the parties, in many instances, will make some attempt to conceal from the knowledge of the court those facts which may be considered as prejudicial to their claims, and that collusion and perjury may well be the result of these efforts. Consequently, the depositions by the parties are ordinarily considered as doing little more than pointing the way to what may be the equitable and just solution of the cause. Their responses, with the exception of those which may be included under the norms of canon 1747 and therefore do not need further proof, must be supported by other evidence before they can be accepted by the court as the truth.[5] To bring to the know-

---

[3]Cf. canons 1708; 1727.

[4]Canon 1742; Wernz-Vidal, *Ius Canonicum* (7 vols. in 9, Romae: Universitas Gregoriana, 1927-1946. Vol. I, 1938; Vol. II, 3. ed., a P. Philippo Aguirre recognita, 1943; Vol. III, 1933; Vol. IV, Pars I, 1934; Vol. IV, Pars II, 1935; Vol. V, 3. ed., a P. Philippo Aguirre recognita, 1946; Vol. VI, 1927; Vol. VI, Pars altera, 1928; Vol. VII, 1937), VI, Pars I, n. 471; Cocchi,*Commentarium in Codicem Iuris Canonici*, VII, 223.

[5]Canon 1747. Non indigent probatione;

1°. Facta notoria, ad normam can. 2197, nn. 2, 3;

2°. Quae ab ipsa lege praesumuntur;

3°. Facta ab uno ex contendentibus asserta et ab altero admissa, nisi a iure vel a iudice probatio nihilominus exigatur.

ledge of the court, therefore, the existence and the nature of whatever proof may be available in order to substantiate the claims of the parties is a further reason for the judicial interrogation of the parties.[6]

It can be readily understood that the judicial attempt to arrive at a just and equitable solution of the matter at issue entails the spending of much time and effort in the searching for and in the examination and the evaluation of proof. The judicial interrogation may be of great assistance in the removal of this obstacle to the speedy and efficient conclusion of the trial. For when, as a result of the interrogations, a judicial confession, made by one of the parties against himself and in favor of the opposing party, is had concerning a point at issue, the adverse party is, particularly in causes which concern the private good, relieved of the burden of further proof.[7]

Since, then, the purpose of the interrogation of the parties is, first, to obtain as complete a knowledge as possible of the object of the trial; secondly, to obtain information concerning the number, nature and availability of the proofs; and, lastly, to obtain, if possible, a judicial confession from one of the parties, this phase of the trial is not only important, but of great practical necessity to the efficient and just settlement of a controversy.

Article 2. The Object of the Judicial Interrogation

The primary object of the judicial interrogation is facts. Not all facts, it is true, but only those facts which pertain to the subject matter of the cause, and which it is hoped will enable the judge to pass sentence in a just manner. For this reason the object of the proofs and that of the judicial interrogations are identical.[8]

---

[6] Wernz-Vidal, *loc. cit.*

[7] Canons 1750; 1751; Roberti, *De Processibus* (2 vols.; Vol. I, 2. ed., Romae: Apud Custodiam Librariam Pontificii Instituti Utriusque Iuris, 1941; Vol. II, Romae: Apud Aedes Facultatis Iuridicae ad S. Apollinaris, Romae, 1926), II, n. 321.

[8] Noval, *Commentarium Codicis Iuris Canonici*, Liber IV, *De Processibus*, Pars I, *De Iudiciis* (Romae: Augustae Taurinorum: Marietti, 1920), n. 432 (hereafter cited as *De Iudiciis*); Cappello, *Summa Iuris Canonici* (3 vols., Vol. III, 2. ed., Romae: Apud Aedes Universitatis Gregorianae, 1940), III, n. 165; cf. canon 1742, § 1.

Two types or categories of fact, the one general and the other particular, comprise the object of the interrogations. The general facts which are common to all interrogatories, irrespective of the nature of the cause, have reference to the general circumstances of the party's life, such as his origin, age, religion, name, residence, *et cetera*. The special or particular facts are those which pertain to the matter at issue, and therefore vary according to the divers kinds of controversies and the peculiar facts and circumstances of each cause.[9]

The object of the interrogations is not the law or points of law. For, as the canonical commentaries contend, it is the duty of the judge to know the law and, in knowing it, it is he, and not the parties, who is to interpret it and to apply it in the individual cause.[10] The law itself is a stable and permanent ordinance of reason for the common good promulgated by him who has charge of the community. Its application, however, in a particular instance will depend upon many facts and circumstances. It is these facts which the judge must know and which are considered as the object of the judicial interrogations.

A more detailed knowledge of the particular law or customs of a place or people may sometimes be necessary. In so far as this knowledge may be considered as a knowledge of facts relative to the cause, they too may be the object of the interrogations.[11]

Article 3. The Division of Judicial Trials

By the term ''ecclesiastical trial'' is meant the legal discussion and settlement before an ecclesiastical tribunal of a controversy, in an affair over which the Church has the right to judge.[12] For an ecclesiastical trial, then, there are required four

---

[9]Canons 1745, § 2; 1774; Roberti, *De Processibus*, II, n. 321.

[10]Cappello, *Summa Iuris Canonici*, III, n. 165; Coronata, *Institutiones Iuris Canonici* (2. ed., 5 vols., Vols. I-II, 1939; Vol. III, 1941; Vol. IV, 1945; Vol. V, 1947, Romae: Marietti), III, n. 1268 (hereafter cited as *Institutiones*); Noval, *De Iudiciis*, n. 432; Wernz-Vidal, *Ius Canonicum*, VI, Pars I, n. 420.

[11]Wernz-Vidal, *loc. cit.*; Noval, *loc. cit.*; Cocchi, *Commentarium in Codicem Iuris Canonici*, VII, n. 129.

[12]Canon 1552, § 1.

essential elements.[13] First, there must be an object which is the thing or right concerning which there is had a controversy. Secondly, there must be contending persons or parties, the one the plaintiff and the other the defendant, who present their grievance to the ecclesiastical tribunal for settlement. The parties are considered to be the passive subject with regard to the trial itself, although in relation to the matter at issue they are the active subject. Thirdly, there must be a judge who, in virtue of his jurisdiction, strives to define and settle the object of the trial justly and according to the norms of law. He is the active subject of the trial. And lastly, it is necessary that the trial be conducted according to the procedural norms determined by the Code of Canon Law and the succeeding instructions of the Holy See. These elements are important and must be found in every judicial trial.[14]

By reason of their object, trials are termed contentious or criminal. Those trials which are concerned with the prosecution or the vindication of the rights of physical or moral persons, or with the declaration of juridic facts concerning such persons, e.g. the validity of a marriage, are called contentious trials.[15] Some canonical commentators, particularly those who dealt with the pre-Code legislation refer to this category of litigation with the term civil trial.[16] Today, however, the term civil has reference more properly to those trials which are conducted be-

---

[13]Wernz-Vidal, *Ius Canonicum*, VI, Pars I, n. 10; Coronata, *Institutiones*, III, n. 1088; Vermeersch-Creusen, *Epitome Iuris Canonici* (6. ed., 3 vols., Vol. I, 1937; Vol. II, 1940; Vol. III, 1946; Mechliniae-Romae: Dessain), III, n. 3 (hereafter cited as *Epitome*).

[14]Canon 1990 designates a number of matrimonial causes in which the solemnities and formalities of an ordinary judicial trial as they are determined in the first section of Book IV of the Code may be omitted. In these causes, the proof of the existence of the matrimonial impediment must be furnished by documents which are beyond suspicion in their veracity and authenticity. This procedure is usually referred to as being summary or extra-ordinary in form, and has for its purpose the more speedy and efficient settlement of causes by means of the curtailment of obviously unnecessary procedural formalities.

[15]Canon 1552, § 2, 1°.

[16]Coronata, Institutiones, III, n. 1089; Woywod, *A Practical Commentary on the Code of Canon Law* (2 vols., tenth printing as edited by C. Smith, New York: Jos. Wagner, Inc., 1946), II, n. 1546 (hereafter cited as *A Practical Commentary*).

fore the secular authority.[17] Criminal trials, on the other hand, are concerned with offenses with a view to inflicting or declaring a penalty.[18]

An offense, in ecclesiastical law, is an external and morally imputable violation of a law to which there is attached at least an indeterminate canonical sanction.[19] Not every violation of an ecclesiastical law is a canonical offense, but only the violation of those laws to which there is attached a penalty. Disobedience to the legitimate precepts of a lawful superior, to which there are added the threat of a penalty, are also under ordinary circumstances to be considered as offenses.[20] The penal sanction attached to the law or precept takes the place of the warning with the threat of penalty which must be given to a person before he can be punished for the violation of a law. Only in cases wherein the seriousness of the scandal or the special gravity arising from the violation of a law or precept, to which there is no penalty attached, demands it, can a penalty be inflicted without this warning.[21]

Offenses which are the subject of criminal trials are those which are public.[22] Precisely what constitutes a public crime is the subject of much discussion among canonical commentators. The more commonly accepted definition, however, following the provisions of the Code, declares that an offense is public when it has been divulged, or when it has been committed under or is attended with such circumstances that its divulgation may and must be prudently considered as following quite readily.[23]

---

[17] Roberti, *De Processibus*, I, n. 57.
[18] Canon 1552, § 2, 2°.
[19] Canon 2195, § 1.
[20] Canon 2195, § 2.
[21] Canon 2222, § 1.
[22] Canon 1933, § 1.
[23] Canon 2197, 1°; Vermeersch-Creusen, *Epitome*, III, n. 258; Coronata, *Institutiones*, III, n. 1452; Blat, *Commentarium Textus Codicis Iuris Canonici* (5 vols. in 7, Vol. IV (*De Processibus*). Romae: Ex Typographia Pontificia in Instituto Pii IX, 1927), IV, n. 477 (hereafter cited as *Commentarium*); Noval, *De Iudiciis*, n. 752. Wernz-Vidal, on the other hand, consider those crimes as public which are possible of proof in the external forum, and against which certain or probable

Essentially the judicial procedure to be followed in a criminal trial is the same as that outlined in the Code of Canon Law for contentious causes.[24] However, a number of accidental differences do exist. Briefly they are the following. Criminal actions or accusations are reserved to the promoter of justice alone to the exclusion of all others.[25] Even though a confession of guilt is had from the defendant, the formal criminal trial may still be instituted in those causes and circumstances which are mentioned in canons 1948-1949. The *litis contestatio* is considered to take place when the defendant replies to the interrogatory of the promoter of justice in the presence of the judge.[26] The oath *de veritate dicenda* is never asked of the defendant in a criminal trial.[27]

A distinction must be made between trials that affect the public good and those which affect the private good. This distinction is of primary importance, and error with regard to it may not only harm the rights of the parties, by the illegal and unwarranted restriction of their private rights,

---

arguments have already been collected with a view to their being proposed in the formal accusation before the judge.—*Ius Canonicum*, VI, Pars I, n. 701.

Wernz-Vidal base their interpretation of the term "public crime" upon the definition of a public impediment as given in canon 1037, which states that an impediment is considered public if it is such that it can be proven in the external forum, otherwise it is occult. Their reason for so contending is that, following the interpretation of canon 2197, 1°, canon 1933, § 1, seemingly forbids the ecclesiastical prosecution of crimes which, while *de facto* they have been committed, still remain occult or non-public in the canonical sense.

Those who hold the opinion that public crime is to be understood according to the definition of canon 2197, 1°, contend that it is true that occult crimes are not subject to criminal procedure (canon 1933, § 1), but that such crimes do not necessarily have to remain occult. For, by means of a denunciation or a canonical investigation *(inquisitio)*, legitimate procedures distinct from a criminal trial, occult crimes are made public and thus become the subject matter of criminal procedure (canons 1934 ff.).

[24]Canon 1959. The delicts, spoken of in canons 2168-2194, are prosecuted in the manner prescribed in the canons themselves (canon 1933, § 2).

[25]Canon 1934.

[26]Coronata, *Institutiones*, III, n. 1475; Wernz-Vidal, *Ius Canonicum*. VI, Pars II, n. 734; Vermeersch-Creusen, *Epitome*, III, n. 273.

[27]Canon 1744.

but harm may also result to the public good by the inefficient and careless vindication and protection of that good which affects all the members of the society.

In affairs which are concerned with the private good of individuals and not with the public good of the society, the judge may proceed in the trial only at the request of the parties, or, since it is a private right which is at issue, it belongs to the parties themselves to decide whether and how far they wish to prosecute or vindicate their right.[28] It belongs to the parties themselves to plead and defend their claims before the tribunal. And if it should happen that the plaintiff does not offer the proofs in his favor which he may properly urge, or if the defendant does not plead the exceptions which he may properly propose, the judge does not supply these deficiences.[29] In fact, it may be said that the court is disinterested and would prefer that the parties settle their differences out of court.[30]

An exception to these general norms is made in favor of minors and those who in law are considered to be the equivalent of minors, e.g., moral persons. In such causes the judge may *ex officio* assist in the pleading or the defending of the minor's claim.[31] The reason for such an exception is the fact that minors are considered to be incapable of properly defending their rights, and thus, indirectly at least, harm would result to the public good if such possible offenses against commutative justice were not prevented by the intervention of the public authority.

In causes which concern the public good, the judicial procedure differs from that which is determined for causes whose subject matter is the private good. In such controversies, since the good of the whole society is considered to be involved, the judge may and indeed must *ex officio*

---

[28]Canon 1618.

[29]Canon 1619, § 1.

[30]Canon 1925; Woywod, *A Practical Commentary*, II, n. 1598.

[31]Canons 100, § 3; 1688, § 2; 1759, § 3; Roberti, *De Processibus, I.* n. 179.

see that all the proofs of the plaintiff and the exceptions of the defendant are presented to the court.[32]

The distinct mode of procedure to be followed in those causes which concern the public good and in those which concern the private good will have an immediate effect upon the judicial interrogations of the parties. For this distinction of causes will determine the right of the judge to interrogate *ex officio*. In controversies involving the public good, the judge has the greater freedom, and must interrogate *ex officio* whenever he considers it opportune and necessary to ascertain the truth of the facts.[33] But, in those causes which are concerned with the private good, the power of the judge is limited. In such trials he interrogates at the instance of the parties, and *ex officio* only for the better understanding of a proof already introduced into the acts of the cause.[34] The importance of the distinction between the causes which affect the public good and those which affect the private good, particularly from the standpoint of the judicial procedure to be followed in such causes, necessitates the following brief remarks on the public and the private good.

Man is by his nature a social being. He is born and lives in human society. He forms an integral part of this society, and as a result there exists a relationship or bond not only between himself and the other members of the society, but also between himself and the society as a whole. But since, in his fallen state, man is possessed of a tendency to evil, it is necessary to have laws regulating his external conduct in order to make certain that the good of the society as a whole as well as that of the individual member is safeguarded. Thus laws are objectively defined as a system or collection of norms, derived from human or divine authority, for the purpose of governing the external actions of individuals, not only in their conduct with other individual persons, but also in their relationship to the society itself, so that the society

---

[32]Canons 1618; 1619 § 2.
[33]Canon 1742, § 1.
[34]Canon 1742, § 2.

may be preserved and thereby attain to its end, which is the good of all the members.[35]

The laws which moderate the relationship between the member of a society and the society itself are termed, at least in the wide sense, public laws, and have for their primary object the public good or, in other words, the good of all the members of the society. The laws which are concerned with the rights and obligations of the members toward each other are designated as private laws, for their principal object is the private good or the good of the individual member of the society.[36]

All laws must be designed for the common good, so that laws which tend to promote the private good of individuals to the detriment of the community as a whole are wrong.[37] The distinction between laws designed for the public good and those designed for the private good is based upon the primary object or scope of the law. For, while laws concerning the public good tend toward their object directly or primarily, laws regarding the private good are designed for the common good only indirectly or secondarily, since by the improvement and the protection of the individual, who is an integral part of the society, the good of the whole society is attained.[38]

Controversies which involve the juridical relationship existing between the society as such and the individual member are considered to involve the public good.[39] Those, however, which are concerned with the relationship that exists between the

[35]Cappello, *Summa Iuris Publici Ecclesiastici* (5. ed., Romae: Apud Aedes Universitatis Gregorianae, 1943), n. 7; Beste, *Introductio In Codicem* (2. ed., Collegeville, Minn.: St. John's Abbey Press, 1944), p. 6.

[36]Cappello, *op. cit.*, n. 23; Beste, *op. cit.*, p. 9; Coronata, *Ius Publicum Ecclesiasticum* (Taurini: Marietti, 1924), n. 5.

[37]Cf. S. Thomas Aquinas, *Summa Theologica*, Ia IIae, q. 90, art. 4; LeBuffe-Hayes, *Jurisprudence* (3. rev. ed., New York: Fordham University Press, 1938), p. 31; Cicognani, *Canon Law* (2. rev. ed., Authorized English Version by J. M. O'Hara and F. Brennan, Westminster, Maryland: The Newman Bookshop, 1946), p. 521 ff.

[38]Coronata, *loc. cit.*

[39]Roberti, *De Processibus*, I, n. 179.

individual members of the society and only secondarily involve the public good are considered to be causes of private good.

The public good is considered by the ecclesiastical authorities to be involved in all criminal trials and in those contentious trials in which the salvation of souls, or the authority and the discipline of the Church as a society is endangered or questioned.[40]

Chief among the contentious causes so considered are those which concern the bonds of marriage and of sacred orders, or which involve the rights of minors or those who in law are considered to be the equivalent of minors.[41]

To give anything like a complete and exhaustive list of all contentious trials which may be said to involve the public good would be a task fraught with many difficulties. The present Code gives an indication of this difficulty. For, while it determines a number of specific controversies in which the promoter of justice must appear in the cause to protect the public good, it is generally left to the prudent judgment of the ordinary to determine this matter.[42] It is evident that many contentious causes may concern the private right of individuals, but by reason of circumstances, such as grave scandal to the faithful, notoriety or the far-reaching effect of the decision, the public good of the Church may be said to be involved. It is this decision which is left to the prudent judgment of the ordinary. Roberti lists a number of contentious causes in which the public good may be said to be involved and in which, consequently, the ordinary would be obliged to order the intervention of the promoter of justice.[43] If, then, neither the law nor the ordinary considers the public good to be concerned in the controversy, it is the private good which is involved.

---

[40]Canon 1618; Coronata, *Institutiones*, III, n. 1269; Roberti, *De Processibus*, I, n. 179; Wernz-Vidal, *Ius Canonicum*, VI, Pars I, nn. 422, 152; Beste, *Introductio in Codicem*, p. 777.

[41]Canons 1856; 88; 100; 1655, § 2.

[42]Canons 1586; 1688, § 2; 1709, § 3; 1734; 1915, § 2; 1971, § 1, 2°.

[43]Roberti, *De Processibus*, I, n. 123, I, 2.

Article 4. The *Positiones*

The allegations were described in the pre-Code legislation as positive assertions of some fact, relative to the matter at issue, which the adverse party was obliged to affirm or deny.[44] In this way, if the allegation was acknowledged as being true, the one who made the charge or claim was relieved of the burden of proving his assertion. Thus much vexatious litigation was avoided by means of an exact determination of what points of the suit must needs be proven, and of what points were accepted as true by both parties.[45]

In a previous article on the historical development of the allegations, the points of difference between the allegations and the interrogations were noted.[46] Briefly stated they were the following: the allegations were made in an affirmative or assertory form, the interrogations were in the form of questions; the allegations were proposed by one party to the other through the medium of the judge, the interrogations were proposed by the judge; the allegations were not used in a criminal process, rather the interrogations had place; and, lastly, the allegations were made with a view to eliciting a confession from the adverse party, while the interrogations sought primarily to investigate the objective truth of the matter at issue.[47]

In the period of legislation preceding the present Code, the terms allegation *(positio,)* article *(articulus)* and interrogation *(interrogatio seu quaesitum)* had a very definite delineation. The term allegation was used in the restricted sense which has been described in the preceding paragraphs. The term article referred to an allegation which had been denied by the adverse party, and hence still remained to be proven during the trial. The term interrogation was used in the restricted sense which it still retains today, of a question, properly so-called.[48]

---

[44]Glossa s. v. *positiones*, ad c. 1, *de confessis*, II, 9, in VI°; Wernz-Vidal, *Ius Canonicum*, VI, Pars I, n. 426; Coronata, *Institutiones*, III, n. 1268; Roberti, *De Processibus*, II, n. 321.

[45]*Loc. cit.*

[46]Cf. *Supra*, p. 27, ff.

[47]Reiffenstuel, *Ius Canonicum Universum*, Lib. II, tit. 18, n. 213 sq.; Coronata, *Institutiones*, III, n. 1268.

[48]Noval, *De Iudiciis*, n. 436.

In the present Code the terms allegation, article and interrogation or question are used indiscriminately and without reference to their pre-Code meaning. Consequently, no special norms are determined to regulate the allegations and their use in the ecclesiastical procedure. In Canon 1745, it is merely stated that both the plaintiff and the defendant, as also the promoter of justice and the defender of the bond, can submit to the judge articles or questions, which are commonly called allegations, upon which they desire him to question a party. The canon further states that in drawing up, admitting, and proposing the allegations or questions to the party, approximately the same norms are to be observed as are enacted in canons 1773-1781 for the questioning of witnesses.[49] Since, then, the Code makes no distinction between an allegation and an interrogation, and since in the last analysis the pre-Code distinction is in reality one of form rather than of essence, the norms for the judicial interrogation of the parties, which are the subject matter of the canonical commentary that follows, also regulate the allegations and their use in the ecclesiastical tribunals. Therefore in the pages which follow no distinction will be made between an interrogation and an allegation, but the general term interrogation or question will be considered to include both concepts.

It may be noted that while the allegations, in the strict sense, are little used today, and that even though the word is often employed to denote a list of prepared questions or an interrogatory, the allegation is still a legitimate and valuable mode of judicial procedure to be used in the search for and the

---

[49]Substantially there is little difference between these norms and those which regulated the allegations, in the strict sense, and their use in the period immediately preceding the Code, namely the procedural rules of the Sacred Roman Rota. There are, however, accidental differences. But when these have been corrected in accordance with the present legislation of the Code, the rules of the Roman Rota provide an excellent commentary on the allegations and their use.—Cf. *Regulae Servandae in Iudiciis apud S. R. Rotae Tribunal*, 4 aug. 1910—*AAS*, II (1910), 783-850; Cocchi, *Commentarium in Codicem Iuris Canonici* VII, n. 132; Wernz-Vidal, *Ius Canonicum*, IV, Pars. I, n. 428.

ascertainment of the objective truth of the matter at issue.[50] In verification of this statement, it may be pointed out that the allegations are still used in the Roman Rota, a court which stands as a model of efficiency and thoroughness for the diocesan tribunals of the world.

---

[50]Cf. Roberti, *De Processibus*, I, n. 321; Coronata, *Institutiones*, III, n. 1268.

CHAPTER VI

THE RIGHT OF JUDICIAL INTERROGATION OF THE PARTIES

Article 1. The Right and the Duty of the Judge

The judge does not make the law. Rather it is his duty to interpret and apply the already existing law, with due consideration of the facts and circumstances, to a given matter pending at issue.[1] To perform this function presupposes on the part of the judge not only a knowledge of the law itself but also a proper understanding of the facts relative to a particular cause. That the judge knows the law is to be presumed, for this knowledge is required of him by the Code of Canon Law before he may be delegated to act in this judicial capacity.[2] On the other hand, however, it is evident that the judicial knowledge of the facts and circumstances of the cause must come from sources other than the judge himself, namely from the parties, their witnesses, documents, experts and the like. As a primary means of achieving this factual knowledge, the present Code, in harmony with judicial procedure down through the ages, determines that the judge has the right to interrogate *ex officio*.[3]

It is the judge who, in a particular controversy, is entrusted with the dispensing of justice and the protection of the public good. Consequently, it is upon him that the obligation rests of directing the entire judicial process towards its proper end, which is, namely, the clarification and triumph of truth and justice. Having established the objective truth of the cause from the acts and proofs of the trial, it is the judge's further obligation to pronounce sentence in conformity with the truth. In this rests the supreme importance and the personal responsi-

---

[1] Cappello, *Summa Iuris Canonici*, III, n. 26.
[2] Canon 1573, § 4.
[3] Canon 1742.

bility of the judge in the direction and the conclusion of the process.[4]

In consequence of these juridical obligations, the judge, in controversies which involve the public good, not only has the right but also the duty to interrogate *ex officio* whenever he believes it opportune and necessary for the search and the ascertainment of the objective truth of the facts relative to the controversy pending at issue.[5] In matters, however, which concern merely the private good of individuals, this right and duty of the judge judicially to interrogate is restricted. In these causes, since they involve a question of the private good, he proceeds only at the request of the parties.[6]

The judge is instructed by the Code to proceed only at the request of the parties in controversies involving the private good, lest he should *ex officio* proceed to adjudicate matters over which the parties have not sought his judicial intervention.[7] The reason is obvious. For if the parties do not request the intervention of the judge, it is to be presumed that their private right had been renounced, or that a satisfactory extrajudicial settlement has been reached between the parties.[8] It is in harmony with the law of the Code that all such controversies concerning the private rights of individuals be settled in an extrajudicial manner.[9]

But, if the controversy concerning a private right has been placed under the judicial competency of a judge for settlement, the burden of proof rests solely upon the plaintiff. And if it should happen that the plaintiff cannot prove his assertions to the satisfaction of the court, the claims against the defendant are to be dismissed as lacking in proof.[10] It is not within the power

---

[4]Cf. "Allocution of Pope Pius XII to the Sacred Roman Rota," October 2, 1944—*AAS*, XXXVI (1944), 281-290, English translation, *The Jurist* (Washington, D.C.: published by the School of Canon Law, The Catholic University of America, 1941—), V (1945), 451-461.

[5]Canon 1742, § 1; cf. canons 1618; 1619, § 2.

[6]Canons 1618; 1619, § 1.

[7]Coronata, *Institutiones*, III, n. 1147.

[8]Beste, *Introductio in Codicem*, p. 777; Cappello, *Summa Iuris Canonici*, III, n. 65.

[9]Canon 1925.

[10]Canons 1748; 1869.

of the judge to aid one party against the other through the introduction of proofs or exceptions. Canon 1619 expressly forbids him to act in this manner. For in these causes the judge is to consider in his passing of sentence only those facts which are presented to him by the parties and their witnesses. He is bound, however, by the duties of his office to see that justice is administered according to the norms of law.[11]

Therefore, with regard to the judicial interrogation of the parties in causes which concern their private good, the judge may interrogate only at the instance of one or the other of the parties. However, since he is bound by his office to administer justice, he has the right to interrogate *ex officio* whenever he considers it necessary and opportune to obtain a more certain and complete knowledge of a fact or proof already introduced into the proceedings by one of the parties.[12]

Article 2. The Collegiate Tribunal

Canon 1576 determines that, every contrary custom being reprobated and every contrary privilege being revoked, certain judicial trials which are enumerated in this canon must be tried by a collegiate tribunal of three or five judges. The judge who is to preside over this tribunal, to direct the procedure, and to decide what is necessary for the administration of justice in the given cause, is the *officialis* or the *vice-officialis*.[13]

The *officialis* is appointed by the bishop, so as to possess ordinary power to judge, and constitutes one tribunal with the bishop.[14] He may try all judicial controversies over which the diocesan tribunal is competent, with the exception of those which the bishop reserves to himself.[15] If it is deemed necessary because of the burden of his duties, assistants may be assigned to the *officialis* with the title of *vice-officialis*.[16]

---

[11] Wernz-Vidal, *Ius Canonicum*, VI, Pars I, n. 152.

[12] Canons 1742, § 2; 1869.

[13] Canons 1582, 1891, 1°; Noval, *De Iudiciis*, n. 126; Lyons, *The*

[14] Canon 1573, §§ 1, 2.

[15] Canon 1573, § 2.

[16] Canon 1573, § 3.

The collegiate tribunal must act as a body and pronounce sentence according to a majority vote.[17] However, the express intervention of all the judges is absolutely required for validity only in the rendition of the final sentence.[18] Nevertheless, the statement of canon 1577, § 1, that the tribunal must act as a body, expresses quite clearly that it is the mind of the legislator that the tribunal should proceed collegiately whenever possible even in those acts which precede the sentence. Accordingly all the judges should be present at each session of the trial, including that session of the trial in which the judicial examination of the parties takes place.[19] When such is the case, it is the presiding judge who conducts the interrogation and the associate judges interrogate, whenever they consider it necessary, only with his permission.[20]

Article 3. The Auditor

It can readily be seen that an inconvenience for all who are concerned in a trial would be the result if it was necessary for the judge in each and every instance to draw up all the acts of the cause. On the part of the judge the onus and the difficulty of being present at each session of all the trials which he is called upon to adjudicate would indeed be great. As for the party, the inconvenience and the hardship of a trial that is being continually postponed or delayed as a result of the inability of the judge and particularly of the collegiate tribunal as a body to be present at the sessions is a fact worthy of consideration. For these reasons the ordinary may, either permanently or for a particular cause, appoint one or several auditors *(instructores)*, whose task it then is to draw up and compile the depositions and testimonies which need to be

---

[17]Canon 1577, § 1.

[18]Canons 1582; 1891, 1°; Noval, *DeD Iudiciis*, n. 126; Lyons, *The Collegiate Tribunal of First Instance* (The Catholic University of America Canon Law Studies, n. 78, Washington, D.C.: The Catholic University of America, 1932), p. 56.

[19]Cf. Cappello, *Summa Iuris Canonici*, III, n. 32.

[20]Canon 1577, § 2; Coronata, *Institutiones*, III, n. 1302; Noval, *De Iudiciis*, nn. 126; 433; Blat, *Commentarium*, IV, n. 241.

gathered in the pending trial.[21] If the ordinary has not already done so, the judge may appoint an auditor to assist him, but he may do so only for the cause which he is trying.[22] An auditor is a priest, who by reason of delegated jurisdiction is empowered to cite witnesses before an ecclesiastical tribunal, to hear their testimony, and to perform other judicial acts in keeping with the limits of the commission through which he acts.[23]

Some canonical authors, however, contend that the frequent contact of the judge with the parties during the preparation of the judicial acts renders it difficult for him to be absolutely impartial to the dictates of justice in the passing of the final sentence. These authors accordingly deem that consideration to be the fundamental reason for the appointment of auditors.[24] Consequently, they conclude that it is necessary for an auditor to be employed for the purpose of drawing up the acts in every judicial trial or that it would be at least expedient to do so.

The premise for the above-mentioned conclusion seems to lack any solid foundation in fact. For it is almost unreasonable to presume that simply from his direct judicial contact with the parties and their witnesses the judge, who is to be a man of irreproachable reputation, of mature judgment, and in no wise connected by bonds of friendship or relationship to the litigants, would be so influenced that he would be unable to render a just decision. Rather the contrary view, namely that through this direct and personal contact with the parties and witnesses the judge derives a greater knowledge of the true facts and circumstances of the cause, seems to be the more reasonable view.[25]

---

[21]Canon 1580, § 1; Roberti, *De Processibus*, I, n. 112.

[22]Canon 1580, § 2.

[23]Canon 1582; Vermeersch-Creusen, *Epitome*, III, n. 40; Wernz-Vidal, *Ius Canonicum*. VI, Pars I, n. 95.

[24]Coronata, *Institutiones*, III, n. 1121. The opinion is mentioned by Wernz-Vidal, *ibid.*, n. 98.

[25]Roberti, *De Processibus*, I, n. 113; Noval, *De Iudiciis*, nn. 126; 135; 433; Wernz-Vidal, *Ius Canonicum*, VI, Pars I, n. 98; Lyons, *The Collegiate Tribunal of First Instance*, p. 60; Cocchi, *Commentarium in Codicem Iuris Canonici*, VII, n. 32, A.

No matter how intelligent or diligent an auditor may be, or no matter how opportunely he questions the parties and the witnesses and seeks to present everything of note to the judge, yet there are many observations, gained in the preparation of the cause, which cannot be fully and adequately presented in the written record. Oftentimes the very character of the person, his condition in life, his voice, eyes, demeanor, and whole appearance manifest much more besides the words which he says, and frequently increase or diminish the force of his spoken word.[26]

It is the judge and not the auditor who is to pass the sentence. Previous to this judicial act, however, moral certitude, which excludes all reasonable doubt concerning the truth of the fact to be defined by his sentence, must be attained by the judge from the acts and proofs of the cause. The judge must weigh the proofs introduced during the judicial proceedings according to his conscience, unless in addition the law explicitly determines the effect to be attributed to certain proofs, e.g. through genuine public documents.[27] The moral certitude of the judge must possess an objective character, and is not to be based solely on the subjective opinion or attitude he may have gained during the trial. Nevertheless, in the evaluation of the depositions and testimonies, the Code determines not only that the judge should consider the credibility and probity of the person testifying as well as the source of the person's knowledge, but also that he should take into consideration the manner in which the testimony was given.[28]

It is evident that, even though the written record of the deposition should contain a description of the person's reactions, mode of delivery, *et cetera*, it is extremely difficult for the judge, from the written record alone, properly to estimate the exact relationship existing between the person's reactions during the examination and the degree of credibility which the judge is to place in the deposition. For example, the acts of the ses-

---

[26]Cf. canon 1789.

[27]Canon 1869; cf. canon 1816.

[28]Canon 1789.

sion in which the examination of the party took place may state
that the party seemed confused or was hesitant in responding to
the interrogations. While no doubt this observation was warranted, personal contact with the party during the interrogation
would have permitted the judge himself to decide whether the
mode of response was due to nervousness or uneasiness in the
presence of the tribunal, whether it was due principally to the
deponent's inability fully and quickly to grasp the import of the
questions, or whether the confusion was the result of a studied
effort to conceal the truth.

In view of this seemingly more reasonable opinion, the
necessity of appointing an auditor to draw up all the preparatory acts of a cause seems not only to be untenable but also to be
disadvantageous to the proper dispensing of justice. Therefore
it is to be preferred that the judge himself prepare the acts of
the cause. The appointment of an auditor, rather than being considered the ordinary and accepted mode of procedure, should
be made only by way of exception.

In those causes which are being tried by a non-collegiate
tribunal of one judge the employment of an auditor should be
rare. For whenever it happens that a judge is too burdened to
conduct the trial in its entirety, a *vice-officialis* rather than an
auditor should be appointed. In this way the *vice-officialis* can
conduct the trial from the beginning to the end without the
need of the appointment of an intermediary between the judge
and the parties.[29]

It is also expedient that the collegiate tribunal, in so far as
is possible, should act together as a body in the preparation of
the acts of the cause. In practice this procedure may entail some
difficulty. When that is the case, then it is to be preferred that
one of the judges, since he will be present during the discussion
of the cause and may at least call the attention of the judges to
the extraordinary happenings in the preparatory stages of the
trial, rather than an auditor, should be delegated by the collegiate tribunal to prepare the acts.[30]

---

[29]Roberti, *De Processibus*, I, n. 113, II.
[30]Roberti, *op. cit.*, I, nn. 108; 113, III.

In conclusion, it may be stated that while it may be true that the preparatory acts of the cause should be drawn up by the judge himself, still neither the Code nor any subsequent instructions of the Holy See have limited his right to the use of an auditor when and if he considers it necessary and opportune.[31]

To the auditor thus appointed for the judicial interrogation of the parties belong the same rights and duties which the judge himself would possess, if he were to conduct the session, unless the tenor of the auditor's mandate limits his power. It is to be noted that even though the auditor may be delegated to conduct the interrogations, the judge does not thereby lose his right to interrogate whenever he considers it necessary and opportune.[32]

One should also advert to the fact that article 88 of the Instruction which is to be observed by diocesan tribunals in the settlement of causes dealing with the nullity of marriage, states that the joining of issue is to be effected before the presiding judge. Thus the auditor is not empowered to effect the joining of issue, although he may be delegated to conduct the judicial interrogation of the parties. Obviously the presiding judge possesses the right to conduct this examination if he so desires. In fact, if when an auditor is appointed the joining of issue and some of the interrogation are to take place in the same session, it appears advisable to have everything in that session conducted by the presiding judge.[33] In this way any confusion that might possibly result if the presiding judge were to effect the joining of issue and an auditor were thereupon to conduct the examination of the consorts is obviated.

---

[31]Canons 1580; 1582; 1715, § 2; 1773; S. C. de Sacramentis, *Instructio Servanda a Tribunalibus Diocesanis in Pertractandis Causis de Nullitate Matrimoniorum*, 15 aug., 1936, arts. 23; 24; 96—*AAS*, XXVIII (1936), 319 and 333 (hereafter cited as *Instructio*).

[32]Wernz-Vidal, *Ius Canonicum*, VI, Pars I, n. 422.

[33]Doheny, *Canonical Procedure in Matrimonial Causes* (2 vols., Vol· I *(Formal Judicial Procedure)*, 1938; Vol. II *(Informal Procedure)*, 1944, Milwaukee: Bruce Publishing Co.), I, 154 (hereafter cited as *Canonical Procedure)*.

Article 4. The Promoter of Justice and the Defender of the Bond

Just as the parties to a controversy are permitted and some-times required to appoint procurators and advocates to represent and protect them before the ecclesiastical tribunal, so the ordinary is obliged to appoint diocesan officials, the promoter of justice and the defender of the bond, to represent and protect the good of the diocese.[34]

It is in the interest of the diocese and consequently of the whole Church that crimes should not go unpunished, that the sacred bonds of matrimony and of orders should not be broken, and that the public rights and laws of the Church in its nature of a fully self-contained society should be protected and upheld. If this were not so, the moral and disciplinary legislation of the Church would be ignored, and the salvation of souls, the primary end of the Church, would be seriously impeded. Therefore the promoter of justice is required to appear in all criminal causes as well as in those contentious causes in which either the law or the prudent judgment of the ordinary consider the public good to be endangered.[35] The defender of the bond must appear in those causes which concern the bonds of matrimony or of orders. He possesses even more extensive rights than the promoter of justice, in order that he may adequately protect these great sacraments from abuse.[36]

These officials, appointed by the ordinary, are to be priests of good repute, doctors of canon law, or at least well-versed in it, and of tried prudence and zeal for justice.[37] The Code of Canon Law emphasizes their importance in a judicial trial when it determines that the acts, in those causes which require their intervention, are null and void if they were not summoned, unless it should happen that they were present despite

---

[34]Canons 1655; 1586; Wernz-Vidal, *Ius Canonicum,* VI, Pars I, nn. 116; 119; Vermeersch-Creusen, *Epitome,* III, n. 283; Cappello, *Summa Iuris Canonici,* III, n. 38.

[35]Canons 1586; 1688, § 2; 1709, § 3; 1734; 1915, § 2; 1971, § 1, 2°; *Instructio,* art. 16—*AAS,* XXVIII (1936), 317-318.

[36]Canons 1586; 1968; 1969; Wernz-Vidal, *op. cit.,* VI, Pars I, n. 119; Cappello, *op. cit.,* III, n. 39.

[37]Canon 1589, § 1.

the lack of a summons. However, if they have been legitimately summoned but are not present during some session, the acts are valid, but they must absolutely be submitted to them afterwards, in order that they may either in writing or orally offer their objections and propose whatever they believe is necessary or useful for the protection of the public good in the cause.[38]

The very nature and purpose of their duties, then, demands that the promoter of justice and the defender of the bond should possess certain rights and duties clearly defined in the law.[39] For if they are to protect the public good, adequate means to do so must be theirs. Among these means placed at their command is that of judicially interrogating the parties.[40]

Propriety in the ecclesiastical court demands not only that the judge moderate the interrogations, but also that he immediately propose all the questions to the parties and the witnesses.[41] Accordingly the promoter and the defender can propose questions to the litigants only through the judge as their intermediary. This they do, for the most part, by submitting to the judge a formulated list of interrogations which they wish to be proposed to the party.[42] In ecclesiastical procedure these lists of questions submitted to the judge are ordinarily referred to as interrogatories.[43]

The promoter of justice and the defender of the bond have the further right of proposing additional questions during the actual examination, in order to resolve any difficulties or doubts which may have arisen as a result of the responses of the party. It is to be noted, however, that even in this event the questions

---

[38]Canon 1587.

[39]Pius XII, "Allocution to the Sacred Roman Rota," 2 oct., 1944—*AAS*, XXXVI (1944), 281 ff.

[40]Canons 1745, § 1; 1968, 1°.

[41]Canons 1745, § 2; 1773; 1968, 1°; *Instructio*, art. 101—*AAS*, XXVIII (1936), 334.

[42]Canons 1745; 1968, 1°; *Instructio*, arts. 70, § 1, 1°; 71, § 2—AAS, XXVIII (1936), 329; Roberti, *De Processibus*, II, n. 323; Wernz-Vidal, *Ius Canonicum*, VI, Pars I, n. 422; Coronata, *Institutiones*, III, n. 1269; Noval, *De Iudiciis*, nn. 800; 801.

[43]Noval, *op. cit.*, n. 431.

are to be suggested to the judge, either orally, or in writing, and that he in turn propose them to the party who is being interrogated.[44]

The promoter of justice has the right to impugn the validity of a marriage when certain conditions demanded by the law have been verified.[45] When he thus appears in a marriage trial, he must propose to the defender of the bond questions which are to be addressed to the parties. The defender must consider these questions as necessary, and is likewise deprived of the right to change them in any way. For the defender has no authority over the promoter in the good exercise of his duties as the protector of the public good. After due cognizance has been taken of the promoter's questions by the defender, they are to be placed in a sealed envelope to be handed to the judge in the actual session for the judicial interrogation.[46] It is evident that the interrogatory of the promoter should be drawn up before that of the defender, and that a knowledge of these questions will greatly assist the defender in preparing his own points and questions for the interrogatory.[47]

In order to lessen the danger of perjury and of collusion, the questions are not to be made known to the parties before they are called to testify.[48] To make certain of this precautionary measure, the defender of the bond, in those causes in which he appears, is instructed to enclose his interrogatory in a sealed envelope and to sign it. This signed and sealed interrogatory is then to be opened by the judge at the actual examina-

---

[44]Canons 1745, § 2; 1773, § 2; 1968, 1°; 1996; *Instructio*, arts. 70, § 1, 1°; 114, § 2—*AAS*, XXVIII (1936), 328, 337.

[45]Canon 1971; *Instructio*, art 35—*AAS*, XXVIII (1936), 321; cf. Bartholemew Fair, "The Promoter of Justice and his Duty to Impugn the Validity of a Marriage,"—*The Jurist*, VII (1947), 378-395.

[46]*Instructio*, art. 71, § 2—*AAS*, XXVIII (1936), 329; Cf. Roberti, "De Condicione Processuali Promotoris Justitiae, Defensoris Vinculi, et Coniugum in Causis Matrimonialibus"—*Apollinaris*, XI (1938), 581.

[47]Doheny, *Canonical Procedure*, I, 154.

[48]Canons 1745, § 2; 1776, § 1; Roberti, *De Processibus*, II, n. 348; Cappello, *Summa Iuris Canonici*, III, n. 192, 3.

tion of the party in the presence of the defender and the person to be questioned.[49] While a similar mode of procedure has not been prescribed for the interrogatory of the promoter of justice, nevertheless the same necessity of guarding against collusion and subornation of witnesses makes it imperative that he exercise due precautions to see that the parties are not forewarned as to the matter of the interrogations.

Not all interrogations can be legitimately proposed to a party in a judicial trial.[50] In order then to safeguard the canonical norms which demand that certain qualities be found in each and every interrogation, ecclesiastical procedure requires that the interrogatories, with the notable exception of that of the defender, must be submitted to the judge previous to the session for the examination. Thus an opportunity is provided for the judge to scrutinize the questions and to pass judgment on their admissibility before they are actually proposed to the party.[51] If the judge should discover that the questions are irrelevant, ensnaring, unnecessarily offensive, or leading, he may correct them or reject them according to his judgment.[52] But in this matter the judge must exercise care lest he hinder the proper fulfillment of the dictates of justice and truth by carelessly and wrongfully rejecting pertinent and legitimate questions.

With regard to the interrogatory of the defender of the bond, there is some doubt whether the judge possesses the power substantially to correct, modify or change the questions contained in it. In fact, the safeguards with which the Code protects the questions of the defender and the extensive rights

---

[49]Canon 1968, 1°; *Instructio*, art. 70, § 1, 1°—*AAS*, XXVIII (1936), 328; S. C. de Sacramentis, *Regulae Servandae in processibus super nullitate sacrae ordinationis vel onerum sacris ordinibus inhaerentium a Sacra Congregatione de Disciplina Sacramentorum editae*, 9 iun. 1931, reg. 19—*AAS*, XXIII (1931), 462 (hereafter cited as *Regulae super nullitate sacrae ordinationis*).

[50]Canon 1775.

[51]Canons 1745; 1773, §2; Roberti, *De Processibus*, II, n. 323.

[52]Noval, *De Iudiciis*, nn. 437; 485; Doheny, *Canonical Procedure*, I, 193.

which are accorded to his office seem rather to indicate that
the judge does not have this power.[53]

It seems evident, however, that minor and obviously necessary changes may be made by the judge during the actual
session for the examination without impeding the right of the
defender. But when the judge feels it necessary to change substantially or to omit entire questions, a difference of opinion
as to the judges power to do so may well arise between the
judge and the defender. Doubtless this will not often happen,
since the officials concerned are prudent men, well-versed in
Canon Law, who are seeking to protect the public good and to
see that justice and truth prevail. Hence little friction should
result.

Since the judge presides over the trial, directs the process, and moderates the proofs,[54] it seems that the right of the
defender to have his interrogations proposed to the party as
formulated is not absolute, and that the judge is able and ought
to change the questions as often as they are manifestly contrary to the law.[55]

If the defender should feel that by the exclusion or the
changing of his questions the proper defense of the bonds of
matrimony or of orders has been unjustly impeded, he may
propose a written objection to the court, to the *officialis*, or
even to the bishop, if need be; but he can hardly interpose a
verbal objection during the actual course of the examination.
Failing in his written objection, the defender may of course
attack the ruling in the *libellus* which shall accompany his appeal in the event that a sentence is given which is unfavorable
to his interest in the cause. If the complaints against a particular

---

[53]Canons 1968; 1969; Roberti, *De Processibus*, II, n. 323; Noval, *De
Iudiciis*, n. 845; Dolan, *The Defensor Vinculi*, (The Catholic University
of America Canon Law Studies, n. 85, Washington, D.C.: The Catholic
University of America, 1934), p. 64.

[54]Canons 1577; 1618; 1749; 1762; 1773; *et cetera; Instructio*, arts. 14,
§ 2; 68—*AAS*, XXVIII (1936), 317; 327-328; Roberti, *De Processibus*, I,
n. 99, I.

[55]Noval, *De Iudiciis*, n. 845; Dolan, *The Defensor Vinculi*, p. 65;
Doheny, *Canonical Procedure*, I, 207; Cocchi, *Commentarium in Codicem Iuris Canonici*, VII, n. 26, d.

auditor or judge are serious and repeated, the matter should be referred to the promoter of justice.[56]

Article 5. The Right of the Parties to Interrogate

In every judicial process there are two distinct parties, the one who is seeking something, and the other against whom or at least in the presence of whom something is sought.[57] In contentious causes the parties are ordinarily termed the plaintiff and the defendant, according as the party institutes the action before an ecclesiastical tribunal or as he opposes the claims of the adverse party.[58] In criminal causes the parties participating in the judicial trial are customarily referred to as the accuser and the accused. In causes of this type it is the promoter of justice who, without exception, is the accuser.[59] Those, however, who have denounced or brought to the attention of the promoter of justice the fact and the circumstances of the crime are obliged to assist him, in so far as possible, in the prosecution of the accused and the consequent vindication of the public good.[60]

Ecclesiastical procedure takes into consideration the fact that the parties are not only vitally concerned with the outcome of the trial, but that they may be presumed to possess a complete, personal and detailed knowledge of the true facts of the cause. Since in some instances it is quite possible that the judicial examination by the court officials may fail to unearth or to verify all these important facts which may have some bearing on the final sentence, the Code gives to the parties the right to interrogate.[61]

Following the norms of law, which demand that all questions be proposed by the judge to the person being examined, the parties are to exercise their right to interrogate by submitting to the judge a list of the questions which they wish to

---

[56]Canons 1984; 1986; *Instructio*, art. 16, § 1—*AAS*, XXVIII (1936), 317; cf. Doheny, *op cit.*, I, 194; Dolan, *The Defensor Vinculi*, p. 65.

[57]Roberti, *De Processibus*, I, 192.

[58]Roberti, *loc. cit.*; cf. canon 1646.

[59]Canon 1934.

[60]Canon 1937.

[61]Canon 1745, § 1.

be proposed to the adverse party.[62] The questions are to be examined by the judge, who then accepts, corrects, or rejects them according as they are found to be in conformity or non-conformity with the qualities demanded of interrogations by the ecclesiastical law in canon 1775.[63]

In the exercise of this prerogative the judge must proceed with extreme care, especially in causes of the private good, when he interrogates at the instance of the party and *ex officio* only to achieve moral certitude concerning a proof already introduced into the acts. And this is so, lest he impair the rights of the parties or create the impression that he favors one of the litigants by his arbitrary and undue restriction of the questions.[64]

Parties who feel that the judge is unduly and unjustly restricting their rights in this matter may invoke the ruling of canon 1625, § 1. This canon states that judges whose competency is certain and evident but who nevertheless refuse to try a cause, judges who rashly declare themselves competent, and judges who through culpable negligence or malice follow an invalid procedure to the injury of others, or do an injustice or otherwise cause damages to the contending parties, are liable for the damages and can be punished by the local ordinary, or, if the bishop has been guilty, by the Apostolic See. The proceedings against the judge may be instituted either at the request of the parties, or even *ex officio*. The penalties are to be proportioned to the gravity of the guilt, and may even extend to the deprivation of office.

In matrimonial causes the questions submitted by the parties are incorporated into the interrogatory of the defender

----

[62]Canons 1745, § 1; 1773; *Instructio*, arts. 70, § 2; 101; 114, § 1—*AAS*, XXVIII (1936), 328, 334, 337.

[63]Canon 1745, § 2; cf. *infra*. p 91 ff.

[64]Canons 1618; 1619; 1742, § 2; *De Iudiciis*, n. 437; Król, *The Defendant in Contentious Trials*, p. 129. "Si vero iudex immerito interrogatorium recusaverit, aderit defectus instructionis, qui substantialis erit prout ius probationis vel defensionis substantialiter fuerit laesum: quod facilius obtinet, si iudex uni parti interrogatorium indulserit, alteri vero denegaverit."—Hanssen, "De Sanctione Nullitatis in Processu Canonico"—*Apollinaris*, XII (1939), 203.

of the bond. He has the right to recast these questions, and should not fail to do so, particularly if they appear to be leading questions. However, the defender is cautioned that he should not suppress anything that is necessary or opportune for the ascertainment of the entire truth in the cause.[65] In the event that the parties or their attorneys do not, of their own volition, submit to the judge questions upon which the other consort is to be examined, they may be invited to do so by the judge at the conclusion of their own examination.[66]

---

[65]*Instructio*, art. 70, § 2—*AAS*, **XXVIII** (1936), 328.
[66]*Instrutio*, art. 114, § 1—*AAS*, **XXVIII** (1936), 337.

CHAPTER VII

THE OATHS AND THE JUDICIAL INTERROGATION OF THE PARTIES

Article 1. The Nature of an Oath

Canon 1316, § 1, defines an oath as the invocation of the Divine Name in witness of the truth. The invocation of the Divine Name pertains to the essence of an oath and consists in the calling upon God to witness and confirm the truth of an oath-taker's statement or testimony. At the same time it implies the acceptance of divine chastisement if an untruth is uttered.[1] Thus an oath pertains to the virtue of religion, and demands the presence of certain conditions before it can be lawful.[2]

The first condition necessary for the taking of an oath is that the statement which is attested to by the oath must be objectively or at least subjectively true. For subjective truth it suffices that the oath-taker have moral certitude, obtained either through his own knowledge or from the testimony of others who are worthy of credence. But in a judicial trial it is necessary that the certitude be had not from the testimony of others but from one's own knowledge.[3] It would be permissible, however, to testify under oath concerning knowledge obtained from others, provided that the testimony is an accurate restatement of the fact, and that the source of one's knowledge be at the same time indicated.[4] Secondly, an oath must be taken with discretion, for it would not be lawful to call God as a witness, without a just cause, for even a trifling affair. Lastly, the object of the oath must be just or morally right. It would be illicit, for example,

---

[1] Vermeersch-Creusen, *Epitome*, II, n. 647.

[2] Canon 1316, § 1. Iusiurandum, idest invocatio Nominis divini in testem veritatis, praestari nequit, nisi in veritate, in iudicio et in iustitia.

[3] Coronata, *Institutiones*, II, n. 901.

[4] Coronata, *loc. cit.*

to employ an oath in confirmation of calumny or of detraction, or to promise under oath to perform some action that is morally wrong.[5]

By reason of their object, oaths are divided into assertory and promissory oaths.[6] With an assertory oath one calls upon God to witness the truth of something that has happened in the past or is now happening, while with a promissory oath one confirms one's present intention of doing something in the future.

The probative value of an oath will depend for the most part on the character of the one taking the oath. For it is true to say that an oath administered to a well-instructed Catholic of unquestionable integrity will be a more evident indication of the truth than an oath which is taken by a person who is, perhaps, notorious for his irreligious attitude. In fact, an oath administered to a person who does not believe in God at all would be of no value whatsoever.[7]

In itself, an oath could be taken by a proxy, but the Code of Canon Law demands that an oath be taken personally by the principal, whenever the canons require or permit the taking of an oath.[8] In ecclesiastical courts, therefore, the oath taken by a procurator on behalf of the party whom he represents would be invalid.[9] The reason, of course, is that, since the oath is concerned with the interior dispositions, the person who is obliged to take the oath is alone fully qualified to swear for himself.[10]

Article 2. The Oath to Tell the Truth
(*Iusiurandum de veritate dicenda*)

The oath to tell the truth, which oath the party takes before the deposition, is a promissory oath by which the affiant

---

[5]Vermeersch-Creusen, *Epitome*, II, n. 648; Coronata, *Institutiones*, II, n. 901.

[6]Vermeersch-Creusen, *Epitome*, II, n. 650.

[7]Woywod-Smith, *A Practical Commentary*, II, 92; Coronata, *Institutiones*, II, n. 900; cf. canons 1757, §§ 1, 2; 1758.

[8]Canons 1316, § 2; 1746.

[9]Canon 1662.

[10]Noval, *De Iudiciis*, n. 438.

[11]Canon 1767, § 1.

binds himself to tell the whole truth and nothing but the truth.[11] By this oath, then, the taker promises to speak the complete truth in answer to all the questions asked of him while he is under oath.[12] He must not be evasive or ambiguous,[13] nor may he seek to employ mental reservations in his responses to the interrogations.[14] Besides swearing to tell the complete truth, the affiant also binds himself to tell the exclusive truth, thereby promising to exclude any element of falsehood from his deposition.[15]

It should be noted that while the oath binds the deponent to speak the complete and exclusive truth in answer to the questions asked, it does not oblige him to volunteer any information which is not requested within the scope of the interrogation.[16]

Before the present law of the Code it was customary to demand of the parties to a trial the *iusiurandum calumniae* and the *iusiurandum malitiae*, in addition to the oath to tell the truth. The *iusiurandum calumniae* was tendered to the party immediately upon the joining of issue, and, in the main, it was an oath designed to prove his good faith in the justice of his cláim, and his intention of avoiding fraud in the actual prosecution of the trial.[17] The *iusiurandum malitiae*, on the other hand, could be demanded at any point in the trial with a view to establishing the truth, not indeed of the whole trial, but of a certain point in it. The primary purpose of this oath was to remove the suspicion, whenever it arose during the trial, that one of the litigants had a malicious intent in view.[18]

The present law of the Code makes no mention of these oaths, and thus by reason of the ruling of canon 6, 6°, they

---

[12]Moriarty, *Oaths in Ecclesiastical Courts*, p. 38.

[13]Blat, *Commentarium*, IV, n. 274.

[14]Denzinger, *Enchiridion Symbolorum*, nn. 1176; 1177.

[15]Reiffenstuel, *Ius Canonicum Universum*, Lib. II, tit. 20, n. 466.

[16]Reiffenstuel, *ibid.*, nn. 465; 468; Moriarty, *Oaths in Ecclesiastical Courts*, p. 38.

[17]Glossa ad c. 1, X, *de iuramento calumniae*, II, 7.

[18]C. 2, *de iuramento calumniae*, II, 4, in VI°.

are considered to have been abrogated.[19] Because these oaths
are no longer utilized in judicial procedure, the importance
and the value of the oath to tell the truth has been greatly
increased. It remains today as a prime means to overcome
vexatious litigation, and to oblige the parties and their witnesses to avoid fraud and falsehood in their testimony.

Article 3. Judicial Norms for Tendering to the Parties the Oath to Tell the Truth

**Canon 1744. Iusiurandum de veritate dicenda in causis
criminalibus nequit iudex accusato deferre; in contentiosis,
quoties bonum publicum in causa est, debet illud a partibus
exigere; in aliis, potest pro sua prudentia.**

Canon 1744 determines the general norms for tendering
to the parties the oath to tell the truth. In keeping with
the established judicial procedure which existed before the
present law of the Code, the demanding from the accused
in criminal trials of the oath to tell the truth is prohibited.
For as the Provincial Council of Rome (1725) pointed out,
". . . no advantage accrues to the prosecution from this practice, and nothing is proven against the defendant by this
custom (as the defendants usually deny the crimes of which
they are charged). So true is this, that not only does no
necessity of demanding the oath exist; nay more, the sacred
character of the oath demands and requires the prohibiting
of the oath under these circumstances."[20] Thus, to eliminate
the proximate occasion of the sin of perjury, the oath is
not to be administered to the accused party in criminal trials.
Wernz-Vidal consider that the struggle occasioned in a man's
conscience between the necessity of admitting the truth under
oath and the fear of the penalties to be incurred is such that

---

[19]Noval, *De Iudiciis*, n. 345; Coronata, *Institutiones*, III, n. 1271;
Wernz-Vidal, *Ius Canonicum*, VI, Pars I, n. 407. The one exception to
this general abrogation is contained in canon 2037, § 4, where the
obligation to take the oath, the *insiurandum calumniae*, is imposed
upon postulators and vice-postulators in causes of beatification.

[20]Tit. XIII, caput 2—Mansi, XXXIV B, 1872; cf. Moriarty, *Oaths in
Ecclesiastical Courts*, p. 33.

the necessitation of it could rightly be deemed inhumanly cruel. [21].

In contentious causes which concern the public good, the oath to tell the truth must be tendered to the parties. The necessity of safeguarding the good of society demands that adequate means be employed for the achieving of that end. The oath to tell the truth is one of the means prescribed by canonical procedure to this end. The omission of this oath would not, however, affect the validity of the deposition or the acts of the cause.[22] When the oath to tell the truth has not been taken, the deposition of the party is to be prudently evaluated by the judge as to its truthfulness, due consideration being accorded to all the circumstances of the cause.[23] It is to be preferred, however, that in this case the oath of having spoken the truth be tendered to the party, which oath would cover the entire content of the deposition, hitherto unconfirmed by an oath to tell the truth.

In contentious causes which involve the private good, the tendering of the oath to tell the truth is left to the prudent discretion of the presiding judge.[24] Since the judge proceeds in such trials at the instance of the parties, either party may request that he tender to the opposing litigant the oath to tell the truth and ordinarily the judge ought to accede to this request lest he render himself suspect of favoring the suit of one party as against the other.[25]

The oath may be demanded either at the beginning of the trial in which case the obligation of speaking the truth under oath would relate to the whole trial, or at any point in the trial, as often as the judge considers it prudent to substantiate some particular point of the deposition.[26] The last-mentioned procedure of tendering the oath during the course of the trial, in

---

[21]Wernz-Vidal, *Ius Canonicum*, VI, Pars I, n. 422a.

[22]Coronata, *Institutiones*, III, n. 1271; Hanssen, De sanctione nullitatis in processu canonico—*Apollinaris*, XII (1939), 204.

[23]Hanssen, *loc. cit.*

[24]Canon 1744.

[25]Cf. canon 1618.

[26]Noval, *De Iudiciis*, n. 435.

accordance with the prudent judgment of the presiding judge, is ordinarily to be preferred. For, according to Noval (1861-1938), this method of procedure is better suited to remind the party of the obligation which is his, namely of speaking the truth, than would be the tendering of the oath at the beginning of the trial.[27] If the oath has been demanded at the beginning of the trial, there is no need to repeat the tendering of the oath during the process; a reminder, when necessary, of the obligation that has been assumed through the taking of the oath would suffice.

Article 4. The Refusal to be Sworn

The law of the Decretals made the party's refusal to take the oath the equivalent to a tacit confession of guilt.[28] Thus the plaintiff, by so refusing to confirm under oath the truthfulness and the justice of his cause, lost his right of judicial action as a dishonest litigant. On the other hand, the refusal of the defendant was considered as an admission of the charges as set forth by the plaintiff in his introductory bill of complaint.

In the present judicial procedure, the party's refusal to be sworn is not necessarily to be construed as tantamount to a confession which concedes the justice of the opposing litigant's cause.[29] It is left to the discretion of the judge, who is to give careful consideration to the motives advanced by the party for his refusal to be sworn, to properly evaluate the party's refusal with a view to determining whether or not it is the equivalent of a confession.[30] Since in a criminal trial the oath to tell the truth is not to be demanded of the defendant, and since it is the promoter of justice who is considered by the law to be the plaintiff, the refusal of the party to be sworn will have application only in contentious causes.[31]

----

[27]Noval, *loc. cit.*

[28]C. 7, **X**, *de iuramento calumniae*, II 7.

[29]Cf. canon 1743, § 2; Roberti, *De Processibus*, II, n. 320; Coronata, *Institutiones*, III, n. 1271; *Instructio*, art. 96, § 1—*AAS*, XXVIII (1936), 333.

[30]Cf canon 1743, § 2; Coronata, *loc. cit.;* Roberti, *loc. cit.*

[31]Canons 1744, 1934.

It may happen that as a consequence of his religious beliefs, e.g. as a Quaker, or as a result of his total unbelief, e.g. as an atheist, or also for the simple reason that he refuses to recognize the right of an ecclesiastical tribunal to try his cause, a party may refuse to confirm his testimony under oath, and yet despite that refusal may be known to have the highest regard for the truth and to be a man of unquestionable integrity. Others, of course, may refuse to take the oath in order to hinder the ascertainment of the truth, in so far as is possible, by witholding from the court the knowledge which they possess concerning the facts of the cause. In all such cases of a refusal to be sworn, a careful consideration of the motive behind the party's conduct will greatly assist the judge in establishing whether there exists a relationship between the party's refusal to be sworn and the justice of the opposing litigant's claims.

In contentious causes which involve the private good, the judicial confession of one party, when freely and deliberately made against himself and in favor of his adversary, relieves the other party from the burden of proof.[32] Therefore, if the unreasonable refusal of the party to be sworn is in such causes construed by the judge as being equivalent of a confession which favors the claims of the opposing party, then the litigant who did not refuse to take the oath needs no longer to prove his contentions.[33] Since in controversies which concern the private good the judge proceeds at the instance of the parties, the unreasonable refusal to confirm one's deposition under oath may well be considered as a confession of guilt which involves the ceding of one's private right in favor of the adverse party.[34]

When, however, the public good is involved in the controversy, in as much as something more important than the private right of an individual is at stake, the judge is instructed to proceed *ex officio* in order that he may adequately protect the common good. In such circumstances a judicial confession does not

---

[32]Canon 1751.

[33]Cf. canons 1743, § 2; 1751.

[34]Canons 1618; 1619; 1747, 3°.

relieve the opponent from the necessity of proving his contentions.[35] Therefore, the unreasonable refusal to confirm one's deposition under oath, while it may be considered as the equivalent of a confession by the judge, does not in causes which concern the public good imply full proof of the adverse party's claims, and consequently does not take away the burden of proof.

Naturally a deposition which is not given under oath is considered of less value than that which is so confirmed. Nevertheless, the unsworn deposition may well be informative on many points which would otherwise remain quite obscure. In circumstances such as these, when the party refuses to testify under oath and the judge considers that the deposition will be useful in the ascertainment of the truth, the party may be allowed to testify apart from being necessitated to take the oath to tell the truth.[36]

It is important that the fact of and the reason for the party's refusal to take the oath should be expressly mentioned by the notary in the acts of the cause. In this way neither the judge nor the other court officials will be tempted to overestimate the value of such an unconfirmed deposition. In addition, the indication of the reason for the refusal to be sworn will tend to provide an opportunity for the proper evaluation of such a deposition in the discussion of the cause. Another reason for inscribing the fact of the refusal in the acts of the cause is that, if the testimony is later proved to be false, the guilty party can be punished only by means of his being excluded for a time to be determined by the judge from the exercise of otherwise authorized ecclesiastical acts. On the other hand, when it is discovered that a person has sworn to testimony which later proves to be false, he is to be deemed guilty of perjury and subject to the penalties mentioned in canon 1743, § 3.[37]

---

[35]Canons 1618; 1619; 1751.

[36]*Instructio*, art. 96, § 1—*AAS*, XXVIII (1936), 333; *Regulae super nullitate sacrae ordinationis*, reg. 30—*AAS*, XXIII (1931), 464.

[37]Cf. *loc. cit.*; Doheny, *Canonical Procedure*, I, 183; also canon 1779.

Article 5. The Procedure to be Followed in Administering to the
Parties the Oath to Tell the Truth

Whenever, according to the norms of canon 1744, the oath
to tell the truth is to be demanded of the parties, it should be
received from them before they are questioned by the judge.[38]

Since the interrogations of the parties may take place at
any stage of the trial until the closing of the period for the
taking of evidence has been decreed by the judge, the administering of the oath to tell the truth may also take place during
this interval of the trial. In some instances, which are determined in canon 1861, the interrogations may be proposed to the
party, and consequently also the oath may be demanded, even
after the closing of the above-mentioned period for the taking
of evidence.[39]

The oath may be demanded in such a way as to cover the
interrogations put to the party during the whole trial, or it may
be concerned only with the interrogations of a particular phase
of the trial.[40] The parties are to take the oath personally.[41]
Whenever there is need of participating in a controversy at
court on the part of moral persons or others who are incapacitated, they are considered to be present in person if their lawful representatives appear in court.[42] The judge, the auditor,
or the delegate is alone authorized to receive the oath of the
party.[43]

As a general rule the oath is to be taken in the tribunal
hall itself.[44] Canon 1770, however contains certain exceptions to this general rule; the persons mentioned in that
canon are excused from a personal appearance in the tribunal
hall where their cause is being tried, and consequently the

[38]Canon 1767, § 1; *Instructio*, art. 96, § 1—*AAS* XXVIII (1936), 333;
Regulae super nullitate sacrae ordinationis, reg. 30—*AAS*, XXIII
(1931), 464.

[39]Canon 1742, § 3.

[40]Roberti, *De Processibus*, II, n. 320.

[41]Canon 1746.

[42]Roberti, *loc. cit.;* Coronata, *Institutiones*, III, n. 1271.

[43]Canon 1622, § 3; *Instructio*, art. 96, § 1—*AAS*, XXVIII (1936), 333;
Coronata, *loc. cit.*

[44]Canons 1636; 1746.

oath may be demanded of them in the place determined by the law for their judicial interrogation.[45]

Whenever an oath is to be taken by the parties, it must always be taken under the invocation of the Divine Name, a priest meanwhile touching his breast, and a layman the Book of the Gospels.[46] In administering the oath to the litigants, the judge should regularly remind them of the sacredness of the act, of the very serious nature of the crime of perjury, and of the penalties to which a person becomes liable if upon being sworn he tells a falsehood in court.[47] When priests and well-instructed Catholics of unquestioned probity take the oath, there is hardly any obligation on the part of the judge to warn them of the sacredness of their act. But one can readily understand that in many instances the character of the party and the deplorable effect of perjury in respect to the party and on the judicial proceedings will warrant a reminder to the parties from the judge of the obligation which they have in conscience to tell the whole truth and nothing but the truth.

Doheny remarks that, in order to effect this warning with prudence and tact, many courts have adopted the method of presenting the deponents with a printed form embodying the warning. This form is read before the party appears to take the oath, and as a consequence the judge may immediately proceed to tender the oath upon the party's acknowledgment of having seen and understood the printed warning.[48] If such a method of procedure is used, it would be advisable for the judge to address a few pertinent questions or remarks to the party in order to make certain that the formula was read and that the party was capable of grasping the full significance of it.

The oath is to be taken according to a formula approved by the judge.[49] The formula may be declaratory or interrogatory in form. In the latter case the judge recites the formula of the

---

[45]Canon 1746.

[46]Canon 1622, § 1.

[47]Canons 1622, § 2; 1743, § 3; *Instructio*, art. 96, § 2—*AAS*, XXVIII (1936), 333.

[48]Doheny, *Canonical Procedure*, I, 185.

[49]Canon 1622, § 3.

oath and the party assents to it. When the declaratory formula is used, the party repeats it, word for word, after the judge. While both forms are admissible, Moriarty contends that the declaratory formula is the more acceptable from the standpoint of impressing the affiant with the importance and the gravity of his act.[50]

In the acts of the cause the notary should indicate the year, the month, the day, and the hour on which the oath was demanded of and pronounced by the party.[51] He should also record the names of the judges, of the promoter of justice, of the defender of the bond, of the opposing party, and of the procurators and the advocates if these persons were present at the session during which the oath was taken. The notation of the name of the party who took the oath, and of his role in the process, as also the formula employed for the taking of the oath, should be duly preserved among the acts of the trial. The judge, the defender of the bond, the promoter of justice, the notary and the party then affix their signatures to this document. If the interrogations and the taking of the oath are combined in one session, one set of signatures will suffice for both the deposition and the oath.[52] If the party should refuse to take the oath to tell the truth, this fact as well as the reasons for the refusal should be noted in the record of the cause.[53]

Article 6. The Penalties for Falsehood and Perjury

Because of the delibarate attempt to impede the just and equitable settlement of a judicial trial, a person who is discovered to have given false information in his deposition is to be punished for his offense.[54] The falsification of a deposition, if it has been given under the oath to tell the truth, is perjury. On the other hand, if no oath has been taken, the offense is con-

---

[50]Moriarty, *Oaths in Ecclesiastical Courts*, p. 44.

[51]Cf. canon 1779.

[52]Roberti, *De Processibus*, II, n. 320; Coronata, *Institutiones*, III, n. 1271; Cf. Moriarty, *loc. cit.*

[53]*Instructio*, art. 96, § 1—*AAS*, XXVIII (1936), 333; *Regulae super nullitate sacrae ordinationis*, reg. 30—*AAS*, XXIII (1931), 464.

[54]Canon 1743, § 3.

sidered as a simple falsehood. The penalties to be inflicted upon the party guilty of such an offense are *ferendae sententiae* penalties, that is, they are not incurred automatically through the very commission of the offense, but they are to be imposed by means of a decree of the judge.[55] The penalties are of their nature vindictive penalties, since they are to be inflicted for a definite period of time to be determined by the judge who is presiding at the trial; the fact that the offender amends and shows good will does not entitle him to be released from the punishment.[56]

A party who has not taken the oath to tell the truth and is later found to have been guilty of falsehood in his deposition is to be punished for a time to be determined by the judge, with a forfeiture of the exercise of otherwise authorized ecclesiastical acts.[57] A party, however, who has confirmed his false deposition under oath is guilty of the more serious crime of perjury, and consequently his punishment is more severe. In the case of a lay person, the penalty to be meted out for perjury is a personal interdict.[58] In the case of a cleric, the crime is to be punished with the vindictive penalty of suspension.[59]

Since the word suspension in canon 1743, § 3, lacks any modifying or restrictive clause, it seems to follow that the ruling of canon 2278, § 2, would apply. That ruling enacts that the effects of suspension are indeed separable, but that unless the contrary is evident, all the consequences of suspension as enumerated in canons 2278-2285 result from a suspension which is inflicted in a general manner.[60]

It is left to the discretion of the judge to determine the length of time during which the penalty will be imposed upon the guilty party.[61] In this determination, consideration should

---

[55]Cf. canons 1743, § 3; 2217, § 1, 2°.

[56]Coronata, *Institutiones*, III, n. 1270.

[57]Canons 1743, § 3; 2256, 2°.

[58]Canons 1743, § 3; 2275; 1757, § 2, 1°.

[59]Canons 1743, § 3; 108, § 1, 1557, § 1; 2227, § 1; Blat, *Commentarium*, IV, n. 242.

[60]Doheny, *Canonical Procedure*, I, 184; Moriarty, *Oaths in Ecclesiastical Courts*, p. 46.

[61]Canon 1743, § 3.

be given to the following circumstances which tend to lessen or increase the gravity of the offense: the importance of the trial, for a greater penalty is deserved by those who impede justice in trials concerning the public good; the influence which the false deposition had or might have had on the sentence; the notoriety of the perjury; and lastly the factors which may or may not increase the imputability of the act.[62]

Article 7. The Oath of Having Spoken the Truth

After the interrogation of the party has been completed, the answers which the notary has reduced to writing should then be read to the party, so that he may be given the opportunity to add, suppress, correct, or change them.[63] When the party has replied that the record of the deposition is satisfactory, he takes the oath of having spoken the truth, if the judge deems it prudent to demand this oath either in reference to all the points of the deposition or of some of them[64]

This step is taken whenever the gravity of the affair or the circumstances of the deposition seem to warrant it. In matrimonial trials and in the process concerning the nullity of sacred ordination, the judge must administer this oath to the parties.[65] In trials of this type the oath of having spoken the truth covers the entire content of the deposition and hence is not to be restricted to a few points. It should again be noted that this oath is not to be demanded of the defendant in criminal trials.[66]

This oath ought to be requested of those who refused to take the oath to tell the truth at the beginning of their deposition, if it may be prudently presumed that they may have changed their attitude during the course of the questioning. In the case wherein the oath to tell the truth has been unintention-

---

[62]Cf. canons 2199-2213; Moriarty, *op. cit.*, p. 47.

[63]Canon 1780; *Instructio*, art. 104, § 1—*AAS*, XXVIII (1936), 335; *Regulae super nullitate sacrae ordinationis*, reg. 37,—*AAS*, XXIII (1931), 466.

[64]Cf. canon 1768; Moriarty, *op. cit.*, p. 57.

[65]*Instructio*, art. 104, § 2—AAS, XXVIII (1936), 335; *Regulae super nullitate sacrae ordinationis*, reg. 37—*AAS*, XXIII (1931), 466.

[66]Canon 1744.

ally overlooked, it may be supplied by the taking of this oath of having spoken the truth. Before the oath of the party is demanded, it is not necessary that the judge once again admonish the party regarding the sanctity of the oath if he has already done so earlier in the trial.

Article 8. The Oath of Secrecy

The judge also binds the parties with an oath of secrecy, if the nature of the case or of the deposition is such that from the divulging of the proceedings and proofs the good reputation of others might be endangered, or if scandal, discord, or other untoward consequences might result.[67] In matrimonial causes and in the trials concerning the nullity of sacred orders, this oath of secrecy is to be taken.[68]

Ordinarily the oath of secrecy binds the party until the publication of the process; however, if the nature of the cause or of the evidence demands it, the judge may bind the party to perpetual secrecy.[69] Whenever the judge wishes to bind the deponents to secrecy for life, he must formulate the wording of the oath accordingly.

---

[67] Canon 1623, § 3.

[68] *Instructio*, art. 104, § 2—*AAS*, XXVIII (1936), 335; *Regulae super nullitate sacrae ordinationis*, reg. 37—*AAS* XXIII (1931), 466.

[69] Cf. canon 1769.

CHAPTER VIII

THE NATURE OF THE JUDICIAL INTERROGATION

Article 1. The Qualities of the Judicial Interrogation

Canon 1775 sets forth in a clear and concise manner the qualities that must be found in every interrogation. This canon states that the interrogations must be brief and simple, not complicated, nor captious, nor cunning, nor suggestive of the answer, nor in any manner offensive, nor irrelevant to the cause in question.

That these qualities should be found in every interrogation appears to be evident when one considers that the purpose of the judicial examination of the party is the attainment of the truth concerning all the facts and circumstances of the cause. The interrogation is never to be conducted with the purpose of confusing the party being questioned, for an interrogation conducted in this manner serves rather to impede than to assist the rendering of a just and equitable sentence. All the courtesies, the amenities, and the proprieties of life should be observed to the highest degree during the examinations. Thus a party is never to be harassed by means of questions which are cunning, suggestive of the answer or in any manner offensive. The high esteem that the Church places upon personal dignity is never to be lost sight of in the ecclesiastical courts.[1]

The interrogations should be adapted to the intelligence of the party being examined, and expressed in the ordinary language of the people.[2] Thus, if the judge should discover that the party is unable to grasp the proper significance of the questions, he should undertake to explain and simplify them. If the question is too long or involved to be kept in mind

---

[1] Doheny, *Canonical Procedure*, I, 151.

[2] *Instructio*, art. 102—*AAS*, XXVIII (1936), 334.

by the party, it is to be divided into parts, so that the answer may be made more easily and more completely.[3]

Canon 1641 rules that if some of the judicial proceedings involve a person who is ignorant of the vernacular, and the judges and the parties do not understand the language of this person, an interpreter under oath is to be designated and employed by the judge. The interpreter should be of such a type that neither party has raised an objection against him. The defender of the bond and the promoter of justice must also be consulted, so that they may be enabled to lodge an exception against the interpreter if they wish to do so in those causes in which they appear.[4] Before beginning his work, the interpreter must take the oath to perform his duties faithfully and to observe secrecy concerning the depositions of the party or parties.[5]

Canon 1775 determines the requisite qualities of the interrogations; however, no precise statement is made as to the enforcement of this ruling. But, since proper court procedure demands that the actual interrogation of the parties be strictly limited to the judge, it appears that he alone is responsible during the course of the examination for the observance of these norms. If three judges were examining conjointly, they would have the right of interposing objections.[6]

Article 2. The Interrogatories

The interrogatories are lists of prepared questions submitted to the judge. On these questions the party, the witness, or the expert is to be interrogated. With reference to the judicial interrogation of the party, the interrogatory is simply a questionnaire upon which the party is to be examined. Its primary purpose is to expedite the drawing up of the process in the probatory stage of the trial. The interrogatory is to

---

[3]S. C. de Sacramentis, *De Processibus in Causis Dispensationis super Matrimonio Rato et non Consummato,* 7 maii, 1923, reg. 31— *AAS,* XV (1923), 398; *Regulae super nullitate sacrae ordinationis,* reg. 22—*AAS,* XXIII (1931), 462-463.

[4]Canon 1641; *Instructio,* art. 108,—AAS, XXVIII (1936), 336.

[5]Canons 1621—1625.

[6]Canons 1745, § 2; 1773; Doheny, *Canonical Procedure,* I, 194.

be drawn up and submitted to the judge at some time previous to that session of the trial which has been set aside for the examination of the party. However, in those causes which concern the validity of the marriage bond or of holy orders, the interrogatory of the defender of the bond is to be submitted to the court in an envelope which has been closed, signed and sealed. It is not to be opened except by the judge at the time of the actual examination of the party.[7]

The right and the duty to prepare and submit an interrogatory upon which the parties to a contentious cause or the accused in a criminal cause are to be examined devolves upon the promoter of justice and the defender of the bond whenever they appear in a cause involving the public good.[8] When the promoter of justice impugns a marriage and as a result both he and the defender are active in the cause, the promoter submits his interrogatory to the defender before the session for the examination. The defender must consider these questions as necessary, and may not omit or change them in any way in the formulation of the interrogatory, since he has no authority over the promoter.[9]

The parties also possess the right to submit questions or to suggest points upon which the opposing party is to be examined and if, perchance, they do not take advantage of this right, they may be invited to do so at the conclusion of the examination.[10] The defender has the right to recast the questions proposed by the party, and he should not fail to do so, particularly if the questions appear to be leading or suggestive of the answer. This is to be done in such a way, however, that he shall suppress nothing that is necessary or opportune for the ascertainment of the entire truth in the cause.[11]

---

[7]Canon 1968, 1°; *Instructio*, arts. 70, § 1, 1°; 101—*AAS*, XXVIII (1936), 328; 334; *Regulae super nullitate sacrae ordinationis*, reg. 19—*AAS*, XXIII (1931), 462.

[8]*Loc. cit.;* Coronata, *Institutiones*, III. n. 1475.

[9]*Instructio*, art. 71, § 2—AAS, XXVIII (1936), 329.

[10]Canon 1745, § 1; *Instructio*, art. 114, § 1—*AAS*, XXVIII (1936), 337.

[11]*Instructio*, art. 70, § 2—AAS, XXVIII (1936), 328; *Regulae super nullitate sacrae ordinationis*, reg. 19—AAS. XXIII (1931), 462.

In causes which involve the public good, the judge is obliged to follow the list of questions submitted to him by promoter of justice and the defender of the bond. He does not, however, lose the right to inspect, modify, and even reject these questions if they lack the requisite qualities demanded of interrogations. The interrogatory of the defender, since it is to be opened only at the time of the actual examination, cannot be shown to the judge beforehand as is the case with regard to the other interrogatories. Rather, if corrections are to be made, they must be made during the actual examination of the party.[12]

The interrogatory submitted by the parties is subject to the same regulations as those which govern the questionnaires of the promoter of justice; although, in matrimonial causes, the defender of the bond has the right to recast them if necessary, and must enclose them with his own interrogatory in the signed and sealed envelope.[13] The examining judge has the right to interpose questions of his own during the examination, and, indeed, he must do so whenever he is of the opinion that the facts, vital to the rendering of a just and equitable decision, have not been introduced into the acts of the cause or have not been sufficiently elucidated.[14]

In causes of private interest, since the judge interrogates at the instance of the party, and *ex officio* only to elucidate proofs which have already been introduced into the acts, he must follow the lists of questions submitted by the parties, provided that they are in accordance with the norms of law regulating the qualities of the interrogations, and forego the supplementing of proofs either directly or indirectly.[15]

The questions contained in the interrogatory of the defender of the bond or of the promoter of justice are divided

---

[12]Cf. canons 1745; 1773; 1775; 1968, 1°; Roberti, *De Processibus*, II, n. 323; Noval, *De Iudiciis*, n. 845; Dolan, *The Defensor Vinculi*, p. 65; Doheny, *Canonical Procedure*, I, 192, 207.

[13]*Instructio*, arts. 70; 101—*AAS*, XXVIII (1936), 328, 334.

[14]Canon 1742, § 1; *Instructio*, art. 101—*AAS*, XXVIII (1936), 334; Doheny, *op. cit.*, I, 192.

[15]Canons 1618; 1619; 1742, § 2; 1773; 1775.

into general and particular.[16] As the term indicates, the
general questions are designed to secure general information
about the party, such as may concern his name, his birth,
his age, his religion, his profession, his domicile (city, parish,
street and number), and his connection, acquaintance or
relationship with the other party to the trial. Each and every
general question is to be proposed to the party at the beginning of the deposition, but need not necessarily be repeated
in the same trial if the party is re-examined. The particular
or special questions are designed with a view to eliciting
the truth about the facts of the cause, and to reveal the
source as well as the time of one's acquisition of the
knowledge.

The preparation of the general questions, since they are
the same for nearly all trials, requires no great study or
forethought. The drawing up of the particular questions,
however, since they are to be drawn up in accordance with
the qualities demanded of the interrogations by canon 1775,
and since they are to serve as an aid for obtaining complete
information about the truth of the cause, including the source
and circumstances of the deponent's knowledge, requires a
great deal of effort and concentration on the part of the
promoter and the defender, whose duty it is to prepare them
for the causes involving the public good.

Article 3. The Place for the Judicial Interrogation

Though the bishop has the right to constitute a tribunal
at any place within his diocese, with the exception of those
places which are exempt, he should nevertheless establish
in his episcopal city a court-room which is to serve as the
ordinary place for the conducting of a trial. A crucifix
should occupy a prominent place in this hall, and a Book of the
Gospels should be provided.[17]

As a general rule it will be in this tribunal hall of the
episcopal see that the judicial interrogation of the parties
will be conducted. Here the parties will present themselves,

---

[16]Canons 1774; 1968, 1°; *Instructio*, art. 99—*AAS* XXVIII (1936),
333.
[17]Canon 1636.

and in the presence of the ecclesiastical judiciary take the oaths that are to be administered, and respond to the legitimate interrogations. However, there are exceptions to this rule.[18] Persons may be exempted from the observance of this norm by reason of their dignity, or because of an impediment either moral or physical, or on account of grave inconvenience.

By reason of their dignity, cardinals, bishops, and those illustrious personages who by the civil law of their country are excused from the obligation of appearing before the secular tribunals for the purpose of testifying, are expressly exempted from the necessity of appearing personally before the judge at the tribunal seat. If, perchance, these persons are cited to appear they are not freed from the judicial interrogation, but they do have the right to select the place in which they prefer the examination to take place. It is their duty to inform the judge of this personal privilege of not appearing in the courthall, and at the same time to designate the place in which the interrogation is to take place.[19]

Other persons may be exempted from a personal appearance at the tribunal by reason of a moral or physicial impediment. Those who are ill or suffering from some defect of mind or body, as well as those who because of their condition in life, e.g. nuns, are unable to go to the seat of the tribunal, are so excused. Their deposition may be taken in their homes by the officials of the court itself, if distance does not render this impracticable.[20]

---

[18]Canon 1746.

[19]Canons 1746; 1770, § 2, 1°; Wernz-Vidal, *Ius Canonicum*, VI, Pars I, n. 462.

[20]Canons 1746; 1770, § 2, 2°. Canon 1757, § 1, declares that those who are mentally defective are to be excluded as unfit to give testimony. Nevertheless, this exclusion is qualified by canon 1758, which states that these unfit witnesses can be examined if the judge issues an order stating that he considers it advisable to do so. Their testimony, however, shall be of value merely as an indication of and a help towards proof of the cause. As a rule such persons shall be examined unsworn. Consequently, in the event that a party to the trial is suffering a mental debility, the reasons favoring an examination are even more aparent than in the case of a witness. For it is quite certain that, unless the nature of the malady renders the examination impossible or useless, the deposition of the party will assist greatly in the search for and in the ascertainment of the objective truth of the cause.

By reason of serious inconvenience, a party may also be excused from appearing personally at the tribunal. It may happen that a party because of great distance connot go to the tribunal or cannot be approached by the judge without great expense and difficulty. While the Code of Canon Law specifically exempts witnesses who find themselves so impeded, it does not expressly state that the parties are likewise privileged to abstain from a personal appearance in the court in such circumstances.[21]

It is evident that the presence of the party in court is more necessary than that of a witness for the efficient and just settlement of a controversy. Consequently the serious inconvenience to a party must be greater, all other things being equal, than that which would be caused to a witness, if it is to justify his absence from the tribunal hall. However, it seems to be the opinion of canonical commentators that if the conditions expressed in canon 1770, § 3, 3°-4°, are verified, the parties themselves may be permitted to be interrogated elsewhere than in the tribunal.[22]

If the party resides in the same diocese in which the controversy is being heard, and cannot because of distance and expense go to the tribunal or be approached by the judge, the judge may appoint a worthy and qualified priest in the vicinity of the party, who shall with the assistance of a notary hold the examination according to the questions and the instructions sent to him by the judge.[23]

If the party resides outside the diocese and cannot without serious inconvenience appear and at the same time is unwilling to approach the tribunal which is trying the cause, then he is to be interrogated by the tribunal of his own diocese if this is possible.[24] If this cannot be done, then a priest and a notary delegated by the tribunal within the jurisdiction of which

---

[21]Canon 1746.

[22]Wernz-Vidal, *Ius Canonicum*, VI, Pars I, n. 424; Vermeersch-Creusen, *Epitome*, III, n. 161; Noval, *De Iudiciis*, n. 438.

[23]Canon 1770, § 2, 4°.

[24]Canon 1770, § 2, 3°.

the party resides is to take the deposition.[25] Generally the notary is to be appointed by the ordinary. However, if in these particular cases no one has been delegated for the task, the priest who has been designated to receive the deposition of the party may himself appoint some prudent person to assist him.[26]

Each tribunal has the right to request the intervention of another tribunal for aid in the completion of those acts of the process which could not otherwise be completed.[27]

It is to be noted that even though the interrogation may be performed in a place other than the tribunal, and by authorized persons other than the judge, the parties are always obliged to respond personally to the questions proposed to them.[28]

Article 4. The Time for the Judicial Interrogation

Canon 1742, § 3, states that the judicial interrogation of the parties may take place at any determined stage of the judicial trial which precedes the conclusion of the period for the taking of evidence.[29] Provision is also made in this canon for the circumstances mentioned in canon 1861, when there is warranted the introduction of new proof into the acts of the cause after the above-mentioned period for the taking of evidence has been concluded. If in view of these circumstances the judge deems it advisable to permit the introduction of this new proof, then the time for the interrogation of the parties is likewise extended.[30]

Whether the judicial trial begins with the citation of the defendant or with the joining of issue *(litis contestatio)* has been the subject of dispute, and was especially so among the pre-Code canonists.[31] Even the present law of the Code is not unmistakably clear on the matter, but when all the pertinent canons are considered it seems that the judicial trial begins with the

---

²⁵Canon 1770, § 2, 4°; Wanenmacher, *Canonical Evidence in Marriage Cases*, p. 61.

²⁶Coronata, *Institutiones*, III, n. 1298.

²⁷Canon 1570, § 2.

²⁸Canon 1746; Noval, *De Iudiciis*, n. 438.

²⁹Canon 1860, § 2.

³⁰Canons 1742, § 3; 1861, §§ 1, 2.

³¹Cf. Wernz-Vidal, *Ius Canonicum*, VI, Pars I, n. 393; Wanenmacher, *Canonical Evidence in Marriage Cases*, p. 38.

citation of the defendant, and is fixed for dispute through the joining of issue, at which stage of the trial there is determined with greater accuracy the precise object of the trial.[32] Hence, when the summons has been rightly issued and canonically served, the judge may proceed to try the cause, after he has abided the time set for the appearance of the parties, even when the defendant has failed to appear in court.[33]

Dilatory exceptions, especially those which have reference to the persons and the manner of the trial, must be proposed and ruled upon before the joining of issue, unless they emerged only after this period of the trial, or unless the party who raises the exception affirms under oath that he did not until then have a knowledge of them.[34] Thus it may be necessary between the citation of the defendant and the joining of issue for the judge to interrogate the parties, and even to call witnesses in order to determine the exact nature of and the ground for the exceptions which have been raised.[35]

If the citation is the beginning of the judicial trial, then these interrogations must indeed be considered as strictly judicial, as also would be the interrogations concerning further incidental matters which may require adjustment prior to the joining of issue, namely, the judicial expenses and the granting or the rejection of gratuitous patronage.[36] The facts uncovered by these interrogations before the joining of issue are of importance only with regard to the settlement of the incidental questions which may have arisen during this introductory period.[37] They may not be used by the judiciary in the formulation of the final sentence, unless they are re-introduced into the

---

[32]Cf. canons 1628, § 1; 1629, § 1; 1631; 1725; 1732; 1734; 1837; Wernz-Vidal, *Ius Canonicum*, VI, Pars I, n. 393; Coronata, *Institutiones*, III, n. 1088; Wanenmacher, *loc. cit.*

[33]Canon 1729, § 1.

[34]Canons 1628, § 1; 1613-1617; 1837; *Instructio*, art. 187—*AAS*, XXVIII (1936), 349.

[35]Werenz-Vidal, *op. cit.*, VI, Pars I, n. 404.

[36]Canon 1631.

[37]Wernz-Vidal, *op. cit.*, VI, Pars I, n. 404, V, notes 16, 17; Coronata, *Institutiones*, III, n. 1255.

acts of the process during the probatory period of the trial following the joining of issue.[38]

When one speaks of the judicial interrogation of the parties, reference is ordinarily had to what may more properly be termed the judicial examination of the parties. This examination takes place after the joining of issue and is primarily concerned with the principal question of the cause rather than with incidental questions which may or may not arise in the process. This judicial examination of the parties takes place after the joining of issue, since before that stage of the trial the exact nature of the dispute has not been fixed or determined, and the intention of the defendant to contest the claims of the plaintiff has not been judicially manifested to the court as yet.[39]

No formalities are required for the joining of issue; it suffices that the parties appear before the judge or his delegate, and that the complaint or the petition of the plaintiff and the denial of the defendant, whereby the matter in dispute and the points of the controversy are clearly determined, are inserted into the acts of the cause.[40]

When the issue has been joined, the judge orders the trial to proceed and appoints a term within which the testimony of the witnesses and the other proofs are to be introduced into the acts of the cause. He should first make some inquiries concerning the number and the whereabouts of the witnesses and the documents, in order that sufficient time will be granted for the proper taking of the evidence. On the motion of the parties, this term for the taking of evidence may be prolonged at the discretion of the judge, but he must see that the trial is not unduly protracted.[41]

In contentious causes that involve the public good, the most fitting time for the examination of the parties is the

---

[38]Cf. canon 1730; Wernz-Vidal, *loc. cit.;* Coronata, *Institutiones*, III, n. 1475.

[39]Canon 1726; *Instructio*, art. 110—*AAS*, XXVIII (1936), 336; Roberti, *De Processibus*, II, n. 321.

[40]Canons 1727-1729.

[41]Canon 1731, 2°; cf. canons 1860; 1861.

period following immediately upon the joining of issue.[42] This appears to be the most opportune time, if one considers the purpose of the interrogation, which is, in brief, the ascertainment of the true fundamental facts of the controversy as it was fixed in the prior joining of issue. In causes that involve the private good, the interrogation takes place at the instance of the parties, and the judge will interrogate *ex officio* only to dispel some doubt concerning a proof already introduced into the cause. Because of this limited right of the judge to interrogate, the examination of the parties will take place, for the most part, during the actual probatory period, when the judge will find it necesssary to re-examine the parties to elucidate the proofs.[43]

In criminal causes the promoter of justice submits together with the introductory libellus a list of interrogations which are to be proposed to the defendant, after the latter's appearance before the tribunal upon his receipt of the judicial citation. The responses of the defendant effect the joining of issue in such causes.[44]

During the probatory period of the trial which follows the joining of issue, new information is constantly being presented to the court. As a result it frequently happens that the entire aspect of the cause is changed, or that there are perceived for the first time contradictions which render it necessary to interrogate the parties anew. This interrogation may in dependence upon the nature of the cause be underaken at the instance of the parties, of the promoter of justice, of the defender of the bond, or even *ex officio* of the tribunal itself, after due consultation with the defender of the bond or the promoter of justice, if these be present at the trial. The request should be made before the acts and the testimonies are made public.[45]

---

[42] Wernz-Vidal, *Ius Canonicum*, VI, Pars I, n. 424; Doheny, *Canonical Procedure*, I, 204; Wanenmacher, *Canonical Evidence in Marriage Cases*, p. 61; Roberti, *De Processibus*, II, n. 321.

[43] Canons 1618; 1619; 1742, § 2; 1745, § 1; Wernz-Vidal, *op cit.*, VI, Pars I, n. 424.

[44] Wernz-Vidal, *Ius Canonicum*, VI, Pars II, n. 734, II; Coronata, *Institutiones*, III, n. 1473.

[45] Cf. canons 1745, § 2; 1781; *Instructio*, art. 107, § 1—*AAS*, XXVIII (1936), 335-336; *Regulae super sacrae ordinationis*, reg. 38, § 1—*AAS*, XXIII (1931), 466.

Whenever in those contentious causes which involve the public good this request for the re-examination of a party is presented to the court, it belongs to the tribunal to reject or to admit this request through a decree after a consultation with the defender of the bond or the promoter of justice. If the request is granted, care should be taken that all danger of collusion and subornation be forestalled.[46]

In the judicial examination of the parties, it is the plaintiff who is to be interrogated in the first place, unless a grave reason suggests that the customary procedure be reversed and the defendant be heard.[47] Dohney claims that the reason why the plaintiff should be the first person to testify before the tribunal is obvious. He has filed the bill of complaint, giving the specific reasons why the validity of the marriage is being impugned in the particular cause. He knows the details of the cause, and can furnish evidence which at least purports to sustain his assertions and charges. He in all likelihood has presented documents of one nature or another to the court when the bill of the complaint was entered. Hence, the defender of the bond and the examining judge are in a position to formulate specific questions for his examination. With the testimony of the plaintiff as a background, the questions for the defendant and the witnesses can be formulated for a definite purpose and with a relevant intent. From this it can be easily deduced why the task of the defender of the bond becomes much more difficult when some grave reason necessitates the examination of the defendant first.[48] While the afore-mentioned reasons have specific reference to matrimonial causes, they are for the most part applicable to all other causes.

When everything that pertains to the producing of proofs has been accomplished, the trial must come to the conclusion of the cause *(conclusio in causa).* This closing of the trial

---

[46]Canon 1781; *Instructio,* art. 107, § 2—*AAS,* XXVIII (1936), 336; *Regulae super nullitate sacrae ordinationis,* reg. 38, § 3—*AAS,* XXIII (1931), 466.

[47]*Instructio,* art. 110—*AAS,* XXVIII (1936), 336.

[48]Doheny, *Canonical Procedure,* I, 205.

takes place when the parties, upon being questioned by the judge, declare that they have nothing further to say, or when the time fixed by the judge for the submission of proofs has expired (provided that the parties were able to avail themselves of the time granted), or when the judge declares that he is sufficiently informed in the cause. The judge shall issue a decree on the closing of the cause, no matter in what manner this took place.[49]

With the conclusion of the trial the period for the judicial examination of the parties comes to a close; it is only when the circumstances determine in canon 1861 are verified that any interrogations may take place after this stage of the trial.[50] Canon 1861 states that after the conclusion of the cause new evidence shall not be admitted, except in causes which never become irrevocably adjudged, or unless documents have been newly discovered, or in the case of witnesses who could not previously be introduced within the proper time on account of some legitimate hindrance. Causes which never become irrevocably adjudged are those which concern the status of persons; but, if two uniform sentences have been issued in these causes, they have the effect that further litigation in court is not to be admitted, unless there be exhibited new and weighty arguments or documents which would warrant a re-opening of the controversy.[51]

Article 5. The Procedural Norms for the Judicial Interrogation

After the joining of issue has taken place in the trial, the tribunal is ready to examine the parties. On the day and at the hour determined by the judge, the party who is to be interrogated appears before the tribunal. If the court wishes, the examining may take place during the same session and immediately after the joining of issue. A judge or auditor, the defender of the bond and the promoter of justice if they are active in the cause, and a notary must be present for

---

[49]Canon 1860.

[50]Canon 1742, § 3.

[51]Canon 1903; cf. Roberti, *De Processibus*, II, n. 511.

the deposition. If the cause is being tried by a collegiate tribunal, it is not necessary for validity that all its members be present, although this would be preferable; it suffices that one of their number or an auditor be delegated to conduct the interrogation of the party.

Particularly with regard to the parties who are contesting the validity of their marriage must the judge take care to ascertain the true identity of the party before beginning the judicial interrogation.[52] Experience has taught ecclesiastical courts that sometimes persons have fraudulently made a substitution for one or the other party in the cause, especially when the impediment involved was that of impotency. The proper identification is to be carried out in accordance with the norms issued by the Sacred Congregation of the Sacraments on March 27, 1929.[53]

The Sacred Congregation decreed the following rules:

1. The officials who are in charge of drawing up these cases must, in the drawing up of the case, diligently inquire into the identity of the persons who are before the court, and especially of the petitioner and the party summoned; and for this purpose they must require an appropiate document duly drawn up by the ecclesiastical or civil authority, which is to be kept in the records of the case, either in the original or in a certified copy.

2. In case the certified copy cannot report all the marks of personal identification which are usually reported in such documents, as, for example, a photograph of the person, it must nevertheless carefully report such marks or identification as will certainly distinguish one person from another.

3. In case such a document cannot be obtained, the identity of the persons must be placed beyond doubt by means of other equivalent documents, or through the testimony of witnesses; and such documents or testimony must likewise be preserved in the records.

---

[52]*Instructio*, arts. 58; 97—*AAS*, XXVIII (1936), 326; 333.
[53]*AAS*, XXI (1929), 490-493.

4. If the judge who draws up the case, or the defender of the bond, or the notary, is well acquainted with the petitioner or the defendant, they shall, without requiring a document of identity, certify in the record to their certain personal knowledge of the party or parties.[54]

In the Matrimonial Instruction of 1936, the norms governing the admittance of advocates *(advocati)* and attorneys *(procuratores)* to the exercise of their office before the tribunal are more stringent than those demanded in the Code.[55] The Instruction requires not only that the advocate and the attorney be Catholics, of full age, and of outstanding reputation for their probity of life and religious character, but also, if they are to participate in matrimonial causes, that they possess a degree in Canon Law, and likewise that they have completed a forensic apprenticeship, preferably at the tribunal of the Sacred Roman Rota. Furthermore, they need the approval of the ordinary in order to be admitted to practise their duties before the tribunal. In view of those prescriptions, it seems probable that, if the advocate or the attorney is well-acquainted with the party or parties, his testimony as to this certain personal knowledge may be accepted by the court as sufficient properly to identity the party or parties to matrimonial cause.[56]

Whenever a document of identification is to be required of parties to an ecclesiastical trial, it is proper to advise them of this need in sufficient time to enable them to procure such a document if they do not already possess one. It is suggested that a notification to this effect be enclosed with the citation which summons the parties to appear for the deposition.

When witnesses are to be used in lieu of a document properly to identify the party or parties, the personal probity and trustworthiness of the witnesses themselves must be

---

[54] Translation from Bouscaren, *The Canon Law Digest* (2 vols., Milwaukee: Bruce, 1934-1943), I, 793.

[55] Cf. canons 1657; 1658; *Instructio*, art. 48—*AAS*, XXVIII (1936), 324.

[56] Torre, *Processus Matrimonialis* (Neapoli [Italia]: D'Auria, 1947), p. 69.

known to the tribunal. If the witnesses are unknown to the tribunal, it cannot be said that the parties have been properly and sufficiently identified.

Following the proper identification of the party, if the oath to speak the truth is to be tendered, in accordance with the norms of canon 1744, it is then administered by the judge in the presence of the promoter of justice and of the defender of the bond, if they are active in the cause, and in the presence of the notary likewise.

In the examination of the party, the questions are not to be proposed by anyone except the judge or by the one who takes his place.[57] If the promoter, the defender, or the adverse party be present at the examination and have new questions which may be proposed to the party, these questions must, either in writing or orally, be proposed to the judge, who will pass upon their acceptability and only then address them to the party.[58]

An exception to the general rule that the judge always propose the interrogations to the parties has been made by a recent decree of the Holy Office concerning the procedure to be followed in matrimonial causes introduced before an ecclesiastical tribunal on the grounds of impotency. The decree stated in part that, after the interrogatories have been duly prepared according to the norms of law, the questioning of the woman in the cause should always indeed take place, but it should be conducted by a medical expert who is to be designated by the ordinary himself. The medical expert should be of mature age, above suspicion, and of solid religious and moral character.[59] The physician himself has the right to supplement the interrogatory of the defender by proposing to the party questions of his own making. He must exercise this right, however, with the approval of the judge and upon consultation with the defender. The notary

---

[57] Canons 1745, § 2; 1773, § 1.

[58] Canons 1745, § 2; 1773, § 2; *Instructio,* art. 101—*AAS,* **XXVIII** (1936), 334.

[59] S. C. S. Off., decr., 12 iun. 1942—*AAS,* **XXXIV** (1942) 200-202.

should make mention in the acts that such questions were proposed by the physician.[60]

While the Code does not explicitly exclude the parties and their legal advisers, namely their advocates and attorneys, from attending the interrogation of the adverse party, some authors maintain that ordinarily they are not to be admitted.[61] Added weight has been given to this opinion by the Matrimonial Instruction of 1936, which states that neither the parties nor their advocates or attorneys may assist at the interrogation of the adverse party. However, by way of exception the judge may grant his permission to admit the parties or their attorneys or their advocates, if the circumstances of the cause seem to warrant this according to the prudent discretion of the judge.[62]

In order to prevent all collusion, all subornation of witnesses, and any and all pre-meditated responses, the party is ordinarily not to be forewarned as to the matter of the questions which are to be proposed to him, unless the facts concerning which he is to testify belong to a period so remote that he could not with certainty answer the questions unless he had time to reflect. In such circumstances the judge may before the examination tell the party to reflect on certain facts, if he believes that this can be done without prejudice to the deposition of the party.[63]

A notification to this effect may be inserted in the document which is issued to the party for the purpose of citing him to appear for the deposition. Nevertheless the manner of forewarning the party is not specified by the Code. Rather it is left to the discretion of the judge. Hence any other suitable means may be employed.[64] The acts, though, should contain some re-

---

[60]Torre, *Processus Matrimonialis*, p. 91.

[61]Wernz-Vidal, *Ius Canonicum*, VI, Pars I, n. 428; Coronata, *Institutiones*, III, n. 1269; cf. canon 1771.

[62]*Instructio*, arts. 101; 128—*AAS*, XXVIII (1936), 334; 339; Cf. *Normae Sacrae Romanae Rotae Tribunalis*, 29 iun. 1934, art. 101—*AAS*, XXVI (1934), 475.

[63]Canons 1745, § 2; 1776; *Instructio*, art. 103, § 1, a—*AAS*, XXVIII (1936), 334.

[64]Coronata, *Institutiones*, III, n. 1305.

cord of the fact that this extraordinary form of procedure was used in the preparation and drawing up of the process. The evaluation of the testimony, which depends in part upon the manner in which it was given, will necessarily be lessened in such instances. Since the party has had time to consider what his responses shall be, his answer will not be spontaneous, and therefore more liable to suspicion.[65]

The answer of the parties to the questions of the judge are to be given orally. They are not permitted to read their deposition from prepared notes or written statements, unless in some particular cause there is a question of figures and accounts. In this latter case the parties are allowed to consult the notes which they have brought with them to refresh their memory.[66] Noval contended that the listed exceptions constitute an all-inclusive listing, so that no other notes may be consulted during the examination.[67] The fact that notes were permitted to be employed by the party should be recorded in the acts of the cause.

Unlike the period before the Code, in which authors admitted the possibility of a party's responding through a procurator in possession of a special mandate, the present legislation requires that the response to an interrogation must be made personally by the party.[68]

Needless to say, the party is better equipped to give a complete and adequate reply. Then, too, there is the added element of judicial evaluation which attaches to one's manner of responding.[69]

The answers of the party are to be committed to writing immediately by the notary, not only in substance but in the

---

[65]Cf. Canon 1789, 3°; Cappello, *Summa Iuris Canonici*, III, n. 192; Cocchi, *Commentarium in Codicem Iuris Canonici*, VII, n. 150.

[66]Canons 1745, § 2; 1777; *Instructio*, art. 103, § 1, b—*AAS*, XXVIII (1936), 334.

[67]Noval, *De Iudiciis*, n. 496.

[68]Canon 1746. Cf. Reiffenstuel, *Ius Canonicum Universum*, Lib. II, tit. 18, n. 245; Noval, *De Iudiciis*, n. 438; *Regulae Servandae in Iudiciis apud S. R. Rotae Tribunal*, 4 aug. 1910, art. 146, n. 2—*AAS*, II (1910), 827.

[69]Hogan, *Judicial Advocates and Procurators*, The Catholic University of America Canon Law Studies, n. 133 (Washington, D.C.: The Catholic University of America Press, 1941), p. 146.

identical words used by the party, unless in view of the slight importance of the answer, the judge thinks it sufficient to have only the substance recorded.[70] At times it may be necessary for the judge, inasmuch as the deponent has a marked tendency to talk rapidly, confusedly, or incoherently, to dictate, as accurately as possible, the party's reply as it is to be entered into the acts. It is to be noted that the Instruction of 1936 gives to the parties in matrimonial causes the right to demand that their deposition be recorded verbatim by the notary.[71] The replies of the party should always be recorded in the first person in the acts.[72]

At the conclusion of the examination, the party's deposition as reduced to writing by the notary is to be read back to the interrogated party. During this reading the judge is to give to the litigant full permission to add, to suppress, to correct or to change his deposition in any way that he may wish.[73] Upon being interrogated in this particular, when the party replies that he has nothing further to state or modify in the written record of his deposition, the oath of having spoken the truth and of keeping the secret with reference to the questions proposed to him and the answers given to them is to be tendered to the party if, in the judgment of the presiding judge, the nature and circumstances of the cause demand it.[74]

The oath of having spoken the truth is an assertory oath by which the party confirms the truth of the deposition which he has made to the court. The oath to keep the secret is a promissory oath and binds the party to keep secret regarding the examination at least until the publication of the process or forever if the nature of the deposition seems to demand this.[75]

---

[70]Canons 1745, § 2; 1778; *Instructio,* art. 103, § 2—*AAS,* XXVIII (1936), 335.

[71]*Instructio,* art. 103, § 2—*AAS,* XXVIII (1936), 335; cf. Doheny, *Canonical Procedure,* I, 196.

[72]Roberti, *De Processibus,* II, n. 349.

[73]Canons 1745, § 2; 1780, § 1; *Instructio,* art. 104, § 1—*AAS,* XXVIII (1936), 335.

[74]Canons 1623, § 3; 1768; 1769.

[75]For a more detailed commentary on the oaths of having spoken the truth and of keeping the secret, cf. *supra* p. 89 Cf. also *Instructio,* art 104, § 2—*AAS,* XXVIII (1936), 335; *Regulae super nullitate sacrae ordinationis,* reg. 37—AAS, XXIII (1931), 466; Moriarty, *Oaths in Ecclesiastical Courts,* p. 57.

Finally, before the party leaves the tribunal, the party, the judge and the notary must affix their signatures to the deposition.[76] The signature of the notary and the seal of the tribunal must appear on every page of the record of the deposition. The signature of the party and of the presiding judge need appear only on that page which records the conclusion of the session.[77]

While canon 1780, § 2, makes no mention of the promoter of justice or of the defender of the bond, later Instructions, in accordance with the pre-Code practice, require that they too affix their signatures to the deposition.[78] It is to be noted that the notary is to be the last to sign the deposition, since with his signature he attests to the authenticity not only of the document but also of the other signatories of the record.[79]

If the party is unable or refuses to sign his name to the deposition, a note to that effect which also indicates the reason for the non-signing by the party is to be made in the record along with the statement that the deposition was read verbatim to the party.[80] The party who refuses to sign his deposition may be compelled to do so through the application of ecclesiastical penalties according to the discretion of the judge.[81] The party, however, who simply does not know how to write, ought to trace a mark in the sign of a cross on the record.[82]

Upon the conclusion of the interrogation in matrimonial causes the *libellus* is to be read to the parties. The plaintiff is to be asked whether or not he confirms it in every detail, while the defendant is to be asked whether or not he contests the accusation contained therein.[83]

---

[76]Canons 1745, § 2; 1780, § 2.

[77]Canon 1643.

[78]*Instructio*, art 104, § 2—*AAS*, XXVIII (1936), 335; *Regulae super nullitate sacrae ordinationis*, reg. 52—*AAS*, XXIII (1931), 469; S. C. C., instr. 22 aug. 1840—*Fontes*, n. 6461; cf. Roberti, *De Processibus*, II, n. 349, note 3, p. 65.

[79]Cf. canon 1585; Roberti, *De Processibus*, I, n. 188.

[80]Canon 1643, § 3.

[81]Cf. canons 1640, § 2; 1766, § 2.

[82]*Instructio*, art. 56—AAS, XXVIII (1936), 325; Roberti, *loc. cit.*

[83]*Instructio*, art. 113, § 1—AAS, XXVIII (1936), 336.

Article 6. The *Confrontatio* of the Parties

The confrontation of the parties either among themselves
or with the witnesses is an extraordinary ecclesiastical procedure. Its purpose is to resolve, if possible, the more grave and
serious difficulties of divergent testimonies already given to
the court.[84] Because it is an extraordinary form of procedure,
the Code requires that it be employed only when it has been
found impossible to reconcile in any other way the depositions
of the parties or the testimony of the witnesses concerning the
major issues which have a substantial relation to the cause. Scan-
dals and dissensions must also be guarded against for if a confrontment would serve only to rouse bitter feelings and
animosities, perchance already existing, its purpose would
be detrimental rather than useful.[85] Coronata observes that
in these circumstances it will be rare that a judge will find
it necessary to employ a confrontment to ascertain the
truth.[86]

It is left to the discretion of the presiding judge to determine when it is necessary and feasible to resort to a confrontment.[87] The judge, however, in causes which concern the public
good, should consult the defender of the bond and the promoter of justice. Upon the decision of the judge, the parties or
witnesses, the promoter of justice and the defender of the bond
are summoned to appear in court at a time designated by the
judge.[88]

Neither the Code nor the Matrimonial Instruction of 1936
determines the exact rules to be followed during the confrontment. The detailed procedure may be similar, in so far as it is
possible, to that designated for an oral discussion of a cause in
canon 1866.[89]

---

[84]Canon 1772, § 2; *Instructio*, art. 114, § 2—*AAS*, XXVIII (1936), 337.

[85]Canon 1772, § 3.

[86]Coronata, *Institutiones*, III, n. 1301.

[87]Canon 1772, § 2; *Instructio*, arts. 114, §2; 133—*AAS*, XXVIII
(1936), 337; 340.

[88]Roberti, *De Processibus*, II, n. 346b; cf. canon 1587.

[89]Doheny,*Canonical Procedure*, I, 250.

In order to suppress all manifestations of antipathy and useless argumentation, the confrontment should be conducted with unusual solemnity and dignity. Before the actual session the judge may interview the parties or witnesses privately, in order to explain to them the exact purpose of the confrontment and the necessity of maintaining dignity and polite restraint during the actual hearing.[90]

At the beginning of the session the oath to speak the truth may be administered, if that be deemed necessary or advisable, even though at the time of the previous deposition this oath had already been taken for the purpose of confirming the truth of their statements. Then the judge states briefly the purpose of the confrontment, and points to the contrary statements that made this extraordinary procedure necessary. Thereupon one party, and then the other, is asked to clarify his statement in order that the truth may be ascertained.[91]

If the parties or witnesses, or even the members of the court, are seriously lacking in the respect and obedience due to the court, they may at once and without further procedure, be forced to obey through censures and other appropriate penalties imposed by the judge in whose presence the offense was committed. Advocates and attorneys who are guilty of such misconduct may be deprived by the judge of the right to conduct other causes before ecclesiastical tribunals.[92]

Upon the conclusion of the confrontment the judge may tender to the parties or witnesses the oath of having spoken the truth and of observing secrecy if the nature and the circumstances of the evidence warrant it.[93] An accurate record of the session should be kept by the notary. It should be signed by the judge, the promoter of justice and the defender of the bond, the parties or witnesses and the notary, and then inserted into the acts of the cause.[94]

---

[90]Doheny, *loc cit.*

[91]Roberti, *loc cit.;* Doheny, *loc. cit.;* Coronata, *Institutiones,* III, n. 1301.

[92]Canon 1640, § 2.

[93]Doheny, *loc. cit.*

[94]Cf. Torre, *Processus Matrimonialis,* p. 97.

Article 7. The Obligation of the Parties to Respond

The correlative of right is duty, inasmuch as right implies a moral restraint on others not to interfere, or a moral constraint to co-operate.[95] The right, therefore, of the judge to interrogate the parties in an effort to ascertain the objective truth of the matter at issue places a corresponding obligation upon the litigants to reply to the judicial interrogations and to speak the truth in so doing.[96] Obedience to the lawful precepts of a competent superior, as well as the obligation which one assumes upon the taking of the oath to tell the truth, constitutes a motive to which the judge can advert in urging upon the parties compliance with their duty of responding truthfully.[97] The obligation of the parties to respond truthfully to the interrogations of the judge is so important and necessary to the proper and efficient administration of justice that the Code is not content to have it understood as a mere correlative of the right to interrogate. The present law positively insists that the parties are obliged to respond and to speak the truth to the judge when he lawfully interrogates them. But if his interrogation touches a delinquency committed by them, they are free to maintain their silence.[98] The obligation, then, which is incumbent upon the party to respond truthfully presupposes two conditions, namely, the judge must be interrogating lawfully, and the question itself must not be concerned with a personal delict of the party being examined.

Not all interrogations proposed to the parties are legitimate or lawful. On the part of the judge, a lawful interrogation requires that, according to the norms of law, he be competent to try the controversy before his tribunal.[99] On the part of the interrogation itself, it is required that its object be a fact or circumstance pertinent to the cause at issue, and amenable also to a

---

[95]LeBuffe-Hayes, *Jurisprudence*, p. 134.
[96]Canon 1742.
[97]Cocchi, *Commentarium in Codicem Iuris Canonici*, VII, n. 130; Wernz-Vidal, *Ius Canonicum*, VI Pars I, n. 423.
[98]Canon 1743, § 1.
[99]Canon 1559.

revelation. Knowledge whose source is a sacramental confession or a professional secret is not considered as amenable to revelation.[100] The manner in which the examination is conducted may also render the questioning of the party unlawful, for instance, if the interrogation, lacking the qualities demanded of interrogations in canon 1775, be proposed to the party in a manner that is complicated, captious, suggestive of the answer, or offensive.

By positive law the parties are exempted from the necessity of confessing their personal delicts.[101] The law does not forbid the party from volunterring this information, but rather states that he cannot be obliged to incriminate himself with his own words. In causes which involve the public good, the judge has the right and the duty to question the party in order to learn the truth, but since laws which contain an exception from the law are to be interpreted in a strict sense, it follows that interrogations which are concerned with a party's personal crime are legitimate and lawful and are not prohibited by the *nisi* clause of canon 1743, § 1.[102] However, if the party refuses to respond, no obligation to do so can be imposed upon him, nor can his refusal be in any way construed as a confession of his guilt, since his refusal is legally justified.[103]

Interrogations concerning personal crimes should not be directed solely and exclusively to the establishment of a party's guilt, but should be undertaken with a view to discovering the whole truth by prudently inquiring into those causes and circumstances which not only lessen one's imputability but even exclude it.[104] This observation has a particular and especial application to criminal trials, since these trials are concerned primarily with the punishment of crime.

---

[100]Canons 1755, § 2; 1757, § 3, 2°; 1775; Noval, *De Iudiciis*, n. 432; Cocchi, *Commentarium in Codicem Iuris Canonici*, VII, n. 130; Coronata, *Institutiones*, III, n. 1270.

[101]Canon 1743, § 1.

[102]Canons 1742, § 1; 19; cf. Roberti, *De Processibus*, II, n. 321; Coronata, *Institutiones*, III, n. 1270.

[103]Cf. canon 1743, §§ 1, 2.

[104]Wernz-Vidal, *Ius Canonicum*, VI, Pars I, n. 422, a; Coronata, *Institutiones*, III, n. 1270.

It is the opinion of the writer that if such interrogations concerning a personal crime are to be proposed to the party, then the party should be advised beforehand that his refusal to answer will not be considered as tantamount to a confession of guilt. For if the party is not aware of this fact of non-obligation, the purpose of or the reason for this exception from the law, as evidenced in the historical development of this concept, is defeated, and the contention of Cappello, that to interrogate directly concerning one's personal crimes is unlawful, while seemingly lacking a foundation in the law, would at least have a basis in equity.[105]

Historically, the reason for the exception enacted in canon 1743, § 1, seems to have been the desire to free the party from an inhuman and almost unnatural dilemma. Since in the period before the Code the refusal to respond was always considered as a confession of the point in question, an interrogation concerning a personal crime placed the party, if guilty, in the unfortunate position either of having to condemn himself or of making himself guilty of perjury or falsehood. Reiffenstuel (1642-1703), in commenting upon the obligation of the party to respond, gave as his opinion that, if the penalty attached to the commission of a crime was very grave, in such an instance the party was justified in denying his guilt.[106] If, then, in a trial conducted according to the procedural norms of the present Code, a party is interrogated concerning his personal crimes and at the same time is unaware of the fact that he is not obliged to respond, his conscience is still burdened with the awful decision of either incriminating himself or of uttering an untruth despite the fact that in law his refusal would not be considered as a confession of guilt.

Sometimes, in matrimonial causes, the decision hinges upon the wrong-doing of one of the parties which may amount to a delict, e.g. on the fact that the party was guilty of abduction, which fact furnished the basis for the invalidity of the mar-

---

[105]Cappello, *Summa Iuris Canonici*, III, n. 166.

[106]Reiffenstuel, *Ius Canonicum Universum*, Lib. II, tit. 18, n. 166.

riage.[107] In such an instance it has been contended that the party
would be obliged to answer truthfully when questioned about
his crime, since it is the validity of the marriage which is really
at issue. The delict is considered as being merely incidental
though prejudicial to the main question, and the party's silence
as redounding to the continuance of an invalid union. The confession of the party could not, however, be used against him in a
criminal trial.[108]

This opinion is untenable since the issuance of the Matrimonial Instruction of 1936. For article 111 quotes canon 1743,
§ 1, in its entirety, and then states that the parties are bound
to reply and to confess the truth to the judge who lawfully interrogates them, *unless* it be a matter of a delinquency committed by them. Consequently, in matrimonial causes the furnishing
of information regarding personal delict must rest on a volun-
tary basis on the side of the deponent.[109]

In the present canonical procedure, the refusal of the party
to answer when lawfully questioned is to be evaluated by the
judge. It is for him to decide whether the refusal is justified, or
whether it is or is not to be held equivalent to an admission of
the claim of the adverse party.[110] If a party who is obliged to
answer refuses, or answers but is found afterwards to have told
a lie, he is to be punished by being excluded from the exercise
of otherwise authorized ecclesiastical acts for a time to be determined according to the circumstances by the judge. If prior to
the interrogation the party took the oath to declare the truth,
he is to be punished with a personal interdict, if he is a lay
person, or with suspension, if he is a cleric.[111]

Article 8. The Record of the Deposition

The record of the party's deposition must be as complete
as possible, containing the fullest and most exact statement of

---

[107]Canon 1074.
[108]Wanenmacher, *Canonical Evidence in Marriage Cases*, p. 52.
[109]Doheny, *Canonical Procedure*, I, 206.
[110]Canon 1743, § 2.
[111]Canon 1743, §§ 2, 3; 2217, § 1, 2°; 2227, § 1; 2256, 2°; 2275; cf.
supra p. 87 ff., where the penalties for falsehood and perjury are
treated.

the facts. The reason for this appears evident when one considers that before pronouncing the sentence the judge must have attained moral certitude about the matter which is to be defined by his sentence, and that this certainty is to be obtained from the acts and proofs of the cause.[112] One must also remember in stressing the importance of a full and adequate record of the deposition that, often in the court of first instance and always in the event of an appeal, the judge or judges entrusted with the duty of passing sentence will not have been present at the actual examination of the party. Consequently any excessive brevity and monosyllabic replies are to be particularly shunned in depositions.[113]

Doheny states that ordinarily the exasperatingly laconic style of the depositions condemned by the Holy See is due not to any terse manner of the witness in answering the questions, but rather to the inexcusably inefficient system of court reporting in vogue in some tribunals. Time and again the Sacred Congregation of the Sacraments and the Tribunal of the Roman Rota have condemned the absolutely unfair and careless abridging of testimony into inane series of ''Yes'' and ''No'' depositions. No court and no notary may in conscience continue to jeopardize the case of a person. This matter is of such grave concern that all bishops and *officiales* should make it their duty to insist that efficient and thorough systems of court reporting be established in their tribunals.[114]

Two things are essential in any system of court reporting: first, an exact copy of the testimony must be made, so that it may be read and signed by the party testifying; second, the transcript of this testimony must be ready for the reading to and the signature of the party before the party leaves the tri-

---

[112]Canon 1869.

[113]S. R. R., *Nullitatis Matrimonii*, 2 dec. 1927, coram R. P. D. Francisco Parillo, Decisio LIII, n. 11—*S. Romanae Rotae Decisiones seu Sententiae* (31 vols., Romae: Typis Vaticanis, 1912-1948), XIX (1927), 481.

[114]Doheny, *Canonical Procedure*, I, 244.

bunal. If these two essentials are fulfilled, courts may employ any system in harmony with the requirements of Canon Law.[115]

In the record of the deposition the notary should mention whether the oath was taken, dispensed with or refused, whether the opposing party and other persons were present, what questions were *ex officio* added to the interrogatory presented to the judge, and generally every worthwhile happening that accompanied the examination.[116]

The notary need not repeat, in the record of the deposition, the questions which are already recorded in writing in the interrogatory submitted to the judge. It is sufficient that he number the replies with the same enumeration with which the corresponding questions were designated. The numerical indication identifies the questions and answers sufficiently. However, the questions added *ex officio* should be designated as such, and written down verbatim in the deposition.[117] Whether these questions were suggested to the judge by the defender of the promoter or the advocate should also be designated in the acts.[118]

The questions are to be stated in their entirety in the deposition, otherwise the exact import of the answer cannot always be accurately appraised. The notary must take care, when questions are interposed *ex officio* during the examination, that the numbering of the already recorded interrogation corresponds with its proper answer, and that the *ex officio* proposed interrogations do not disrupt this order.

Any unusual features occurring during the examination, such as hesitancy, change of attitude, inconstant retracting and correcting of answers, and other indications which may prove to be of assistance to the judge in forming an opinion regarding

---

[115]Doheny, *op. cit.*, I, 197.

[116]Canon 1779.

[117]S. C. de Sacramentis, *Regulae Servandae in Processibus super Matrimonio Rato et non Consummato*, 7 maii, 1923, reg. 44, § 3—*AAS*, XV (1923), 401-402; Roberti, *De Processibus*, II, n. 349.

[118]Torre,*Processus Matrimonialis*, p. 77.

the party's sincerity and knowledge should also be recorded in the deposition.[119]

---

[119]Canons 1745, § 2; 1779; Wernz-Vidal, *Ius Canonicum*, VI, Pars I, n. 473; Roberti, *loc. cit.;* Vaughan, *Constitutions for Diocesan Courts*, The Catholic University of America Canon Law Studies, n. 210 (Washington, D. C.: The Catholic University of America Press, 1944), p. 87.

CONCLUSIONS

1. With regard to the legal development of the procedural norms for the judicial interrogation of the parties it may be stated that:

a) Historically there appears very little canonical legislation concerning the interrogation of the parties until the 19th century. In great part this was probably due to the fact that Roman Law legislation, a supplementary source for the Ecclesiastical Law, was considered as adequate on this phase of procedure. This assumption is seemingly verified by the fact that most of the glosses, which make reference to this matter in the Decretal Collections, offered merely a summary of the pertinent passages of Roman Law.

b) It was not until the Sacred Congregation of the Council issued the well-known Instruction *Cum moneat Glossa*, in 1840, that the judicial interrogation of the parties became part of the written law of the Church.

c) The procedural rules of the Sacred Roman Rota (1910) are the primary source from which has been borrowed the universal procedural law of today. This statement is particularly true with regard to the judicial interrogation of the parties.

2. The opinion which states that an auditor must be appointed to draw up all the preparatory acts of a trial is not only untenable but also disadvantageous to the proper dispensing of justice.

3. The right of the defender of the bond to have his interrogatory proposed to the party is not absolute. The judge is able and ought to modify and correct the questions as often as they are manifestly opposed to the law. The right of the judge so to act is, however, limited to the time of the actual session of the trial, since the interrogatory of the defender being en-

closed, signed and contained in a sealed envelope, is not opened until the session for the interrogation begins.

4. Interrogations concerning a party's personal delicts are lawful. The party is not obliged to respond to these interrogations, nor is his refusal to be construed as an admission of guilt. It is advisable that the party be forewarned of this privilege, which is his in law, of not responding.

BIBLIOGRAPHY

Sources

Acta Apostolicae Sedis, Commentarium Officiale, Romae, 1909—

Acta Sancta Sedis, 41 vols., Romae, 1865-1908.

Canones et Decreta Sacrosancti Oecumenici Concilii Tridentini, Taurini: Marietti, 1913.

Codex Theodosianus, ed. P. Krueger, T. Mommsen, 3 vols., Berolini, *dicti Papae XV auctoritate promulgatus*, Romae: Typis Polyglottis Vaticanis, 1917.

Codex Theodosianus, ed. P. Krueger, T. Mommsen, 3 vols., Bereolini, 1905.

Codicis Iuris Canonici Fontes cura Emi Petri Card. Gasparri editi, 9 vols., Romae (postea Civitate Vaticana): Typis Polyglottis, 1923-1939 (Vols. VII-IX, ed. cura et studio Emi Iustiniani Card. Serédi).

Collectanea S. Congregationis de Propaganda Fide, 2 vols., Romae: Typographia Polyglotta S. C. de Prop. Fide, 1907.

Corpus Iuris Canonici, ed. Lipsiensis 2., Aemilius Richter-Aemilius Friedberg, 2 vols., Lipsiae: Tauchnitz, 1879-1881.

Corpus Iuris Civilis, Vol. I, *Institutiones*, ed. stereotypa 15.—recognovit P. Krueger; Vol. I, *Digesta*, ed. stereotypa 15.— recognovit T. Mommsen, retractavit P. Krueger; Vol. II, *Codex Instinianus, ed.* stereotypa 10.—recognovit et retractavit P. Krueger; Vol. III, *Novellae Constitutiones*, ed. stereotypa 5.—recognovit R. Schoell; opus Schoellii morte interceptum absolvit G. Kroll, Berolini: apud Weidmannos, 1928-1929.

Decretales D. Gregorii Papae IX, una cum Glossis Restitutae, Romae, 1582.

Enchiridion Symbolorum, Definitionum, et Declarationum de Rebus Fidei et Morum, ed, H. Denzinger-C. Bannwart—J. B. Umberg, 21-23 ed., Friburgi Brisgoviae: Herder & Co., 1937.

Hinschius, Paulus, *Decretales Pseudo-Isidorianae et Capitula Angilramni, Lipsiae*, 1863.

Jaffé, Philippus, *Regesta Pontificum Romanorum ab condita Ecclesia ad annum post Christum natum MCXCVIII*, 2. ed., correctam et auctam auspiciis Gulielmi Wattenbach, curaverunt S. Loewenfeld, F. Kaltenbrunner, P. Ewald, 2 vols. in 1, Lipsiae, 1885-1888.

Liber Sextus Decretalium, una cum Clementinis et Extravagantibus earumque glossis restitutis, Romae, 1582.

Mansi, Joannes D., *Sacrorum Conciliorum Nova et Amplissima Collectio*, 53 vols. in 60, Paris-Leipzig-Arnhem, 1901-1927.

Migne, J. P., *Patrologiae Cursus Completus, Series Latina*, 221 vols., Parisiis, 1844-1855.

Monumenta Germaniae Historica, Epistolarum Tomus I et II, edd. P. Ewald et L. Hartmann, Berolini: Apud Weidmannos, 1891-1899.

Sacrae Romanae Rotae Decisiones seu Sententia (ab anno 1909), Romae: Typis Vaticanis, 1912—.

Schroeder, H. J., *Canons and Decrees of the Council of Trent*, St. Louis: B. Herder & Co., 1941.

Reference Works

Aquinas, St. Thomas, *Summa Theologica*, editio Emi Josepho Card. Pecci oblata, 6 vols., Parisiis, 1941.

Beste, Udalricus, *Introductio in Codicem*, 2 ed., Collegeville, Minn.: St. John's Abbey Press, 1944.

Blat, Albertus, *Commentarium Textus Codicis Iuris Canonici*, 5 vols. in 7, Vol. IV, *De Processibus*, Romae: Ex Typographia Pontificia in Instituto Pii X, 1927.

Bouix, M. D., *Tractatus de Iudiciis Ecclesiasticis*, 2 vols. in 1, Parisiis, 1855.

Bouscaren, T. L., *The Canon Law Digest*, 2 vols., Milwaukee: Bruce, 1934-1943.

Buckland, W. W., *A Manual of Roman Private Law*, Cambridge: Cambridge University Press, 1925.

————*A Text Book of Roman Law from Augustus to Justinian*, 2. ed., Cambridge: Cambridge University Press, 1932.

Cappello, Felix, *Summa Iuris Publici Ecclesiastici*, 5. ed., Romae: Apud Aedes Universitatis Gregorianae, 1943.

————*Summa Iuris Canonici*, 3 vols., Vol. III, 2. ed., Romae: Apud Aedes Universitatis Gregorianae, 1940.

Catholic Encyclopedia, The, 15 vols., Index and 2 Supplements, New York, 1907-1922.

Cicognani, Amleto, *Canon Law*, 2. rev. ed., Authorized English Version by J. M. O'Hara and F. Brennan, Westminster, Maryland: The Newman Bookshop, 1946.

Cocchi, Guidus, *Commentarium in Codicem Iuris Canonici*, 8 vols. in 5, Vol. VII, De Processibus, 4. ed., Augustae: Marietti, 1940.

Coronata, M., *Institutiones Iuris Canonici*, 2. ed., 5 vols., Vols. I-II, 1939; Vol. III, 1941; Vol. IV, 1945; Vol. V, 1947, Romae: Marietti.

————*Ius Publicum Ecclesiasticum*, Taurini: Marietti, 1924.

DeAngelis, P., *Praelectiones Iuris Canonici*, 5 vols. in 9, Romae, 1877-1891.

Doheny, William, J., *Canonical Procedure in Matrimonial Cases*, 2 vols. Vol. I, *Formal Judicial Procedure*, 1938; Vol. II, *Informal Procedure*, 1944, Milwaukee: Bruce Publishing Co.

Dolan, J., *The Defensor Vinculi*, The Catholic University of America, Canon Law Studies, n. 85, Washington, D. C.: The Catholic University of America, 1934.

Droste, F.—Messmer, S. C., *Canonical Procedure in Criminal and Disciplinary Cases of Clerics*, New York, 1897.

Durantis, Gulielmus, *Speculum Iuris*, 3 vols., Venetiis, 1577.

Engelmann, A., *A History of Continental Civil Procedure*, translated by R. W. Millar, Boston: Little, Brown & Co., 1927; Vol. VII of *The Continental Legal Series*, 10 vols.

Esmein, A., *A History of Continental Criminal Procedure*, translated by J. Simpson, Boston: Little, Brown & Co., 1913; Vol. V. of *The Continental Legal Series*, 10 vols.

Fagnanus, P., *Commentaria in Quinque Libros Decretalium*, 3 vols., Venetiis, 1729.

Glynn, J. C., *The Promoter of Justice*, The Catholic University of America Canon Law Studies, n. 101, Washington, D.C.: The Catholic University of America, 1936.

Hogan, J. J., *Judicial Advocates and Procurators*, The Catholic University of America Canon Law Studies, n. 133, Washington, D.C.: The Catholic University of America Press, 1941.

Hostiensis, Cardinalis (Henricus de Segusio), *Commentaria in Quinque Decretalium Libros*, 5 vols. in 3, Venetiis, 1581.

————*Summa Aurea*, Lugduni, 1568.

Król, J. J., *The Defendant in Ecclesiastical Trials*, The Catholic University of America Canon Law Studies, n. 146, Washington, D.C.: The Catholic University of America Press, 1942.

Jolowicz, H. F., *Historical Introduction to the Study of Roman Law*, Cambridge: Cambridge University Press, 1932.

Kealy, J. J., *The Introductory Libellus in Church Court Procedure*, The Catholic University of America Canon Law Studies, n. 108, Washington, D.C.: The Catholic University of America, 1937.

LeBuffe, F.—Hayes, James, *Jurisprudence*, 3. rev. ed., New York: Fordham University Press, 1938.

Lyons, Avitus, *The Collegiate Tribunal of First Instance*, The Catholic University of America Canon Law Studies, n. 78, Washington, D.C.: The Catholic University of America, 1932.

Moriarty, E. J., *Oaths in Ecclesiastical Courts*, The Catholic University of America Canon Law Studies, n. 110, Washington, D.C.: The Catholic University of America, 1937.

Muirhead, J., *Roman Law*, London, 1899.

Noval, J., *Commentarium Codicis Iuris Canonici*, Lib. IV, *De Processibus*, pars I, *De Iudiciis*, Augustae Taurinorum: Marietti, 1920.

Ottaviani, A., *Institutiones Iuris Publici Ecclesiastici*, 2. ed., 2 vols., Civitate Vaticana: Typis Polyglottis, 1935-1936.

Panormitanus (Nicholas de Tudeschis), *Commentaria in Quinque Libros Decretalium*, 5 vols. in 7, Venetiis, 1588.

Pirhing, E., *Jus Canonicum in Quinque Libros Decretalium*, 5 vols., Dilingae, 1674-1678.

Reiffenstuel, Anacletus, *Ius Canonicum Universum*, 5 vols. in 7, Parisiis, 1864-1870.

Roberti, Franciscus, *De Processibus*, 2 vols., Vol. I, 2. ed., Romae: Apud Custodiam Librariam Pontificii Instituti Utriusque Iuris, 1941; Vol. II, Romae: Apud Aedes Facultatis Iuridicae ad S. Apollinaris,, Romae, 1926.

Roby, H. J., *Roman Private Law*, 2 vols., Cambridge: Cambridge University Press, 1902.

Rufinus, *Summa Decretorum*, ed. H. Singer, Paderborn, 1902.

Santi, F. *Praelectiones Iuris Canonici iuxta Ordinem Decretalium Gregorii IX*. 2 vols., Ratisbonae, 1886.

Schmalzgrueber, F., *Ius Ecclesiasticum Universum*, 5 vols in 12, Romae: ex Typographia Rev. Cam. Apostolicae, 1843-1845.

Scott, S. P., *The Civil Law*, a Translation of the Code of Justinian, 14 vols., Philadelphia: The Central Trust Co., 1932.

Sherman, C. P., *Roman Law in the Modern World*, 2. ed., 3 vols., New York: Baker, Voorhis & Co., 1924.

Smith, S. B., *Elements of Ecclesiastical Law*, 3 vols., Vol. II, *Ecclesiastical Trials*, 5. ed., New York: Benziger Bros., 1887.

————*New Procedure in Criminal and Disciplinary Causes of Ecclesiastics in the United States*, 3. ed., New York, 1898.

Torre, J., *Processus Matrimonialis*, Neapoli (Italia): D'Auria, 1947.

Tuberville, A. S., *The Spanish Inquisition*, London: Thornton Butterworth, Limited, 1932.

Van Hove, A., *Commentarium Lovaniense in Codicem Iuris Canonici*, Vol. I, Tom. I, *Prolegomena ad Codicem Iuris Canonici*, 2. ed., Mechliniae-Romae: H. Dessain, 1945.

Vaughan, *Constitutions for Diocesan Courts*, The Catholic University of America Canon Law Studies, n. 210 Washington, D.C.: The Catholic University of America Press, 1944.

Vecchiotti, S. M., *Institutiones Canonicae*, 16. ed., 3 vols., Augustae Taurinorum, 1875.

Vermeersch, A.—Creusen, J., *Epitome Iuris Canonici*, 6. ed., 3 vols., Mechliniae-Romae: H. Dessain, 1937-1946.

Von Bar, C. L., *A History of Continental Criminal Law*, translated by Thomas S. Bell, Boston: Little, Brown & Co., 1916; Vol. IV of *The Continental Legal Series*, 10 vols.

Wanenmacher, F., *Canonical Evidence in Marriage Cases*, Philadelphia: The Dolphin Press, 1935.

Wernz, F. X., *Ius Decretalium*, 6 vols., 2. ed., Romae et Prati, 1906-1913.

————, Vidal, P., *Ius Canonicum*, 7 vols. in 9, Romae: Universitas Gregoriana, 1927-1946, Vol. I, 1938; Vol. II, 3. ed., a P. Philippo Aguirre recognita, 1943; Vol. III, 1933; Vol. IV, Pars I, 1934; Vol. IV, Pars II, 1935; Vol. V, 3. ed., a P. Philippo Aguirre recognita, 1946; Vol. VI, 1927; Vol. VI, Pars Altera, 1928; Vol. VII, 1937.

Woywod, S., *A Practical Commentary on the Code of Canon Law*, 2 vols., tenth printing as edited by C. Smith, New York: J. Wagner, Inc., 1946.

Articles

Bernardini, C., "Normae S. R. Rotae"—*Apollinaris*, VII (1934), 429-478.

Broderick, J., "Ought Catholics to Defend the Inquisition?"—*The Month*, CLXXVII (1941), 118-123.

Fair, B., "The Promoter of Juustice and his Duty to Impugn the Validity of a Marriage"—*The Jurist*, VII (1947), 378-395.

Hanssen, A., "De Sanctione Nullitatis in Processu Canonico"—*Apollinaris*, XI (1938), 71-109; 215-263; 381-403; XII (1939), 198-251.

Ojetti, B., "Ecclesiastical Courts"—*Catholic Encyclopedia*, IV, 447-453.

Pius XII, Pope, "Allocution to the Sacred Roman Rota"—*AAS*, XXXVI (1944). 281-290—*The Jurist*, V (1945), 451-461.

Roberti, F., "De Condicione Processuali Promotoris Institiae, Defensoris Vinculi, et Coniugum in Causis Matrimonialibus"—*Apollinaris*, XI (1938), 575-584.

Periodicals

Analecta Iuris Pontificii, 28 vols., Romae. 1855-1869; Parisiis, 1872-1891.

Apollinaris, Romae, 1928—

Jurist, The, Washington, D.C., 1941—

Month, The, London, 1864—

Abbreviations

AAS—Acta Apostolicae Sedis

ASS—Acta Sanctae Sedis

C.—Codex Iustinianus

C. Th.—Codex Theodosianus

D.—Digesta

Fontes—Codicis Iuris Canonici Fontes cura......Gasparri editi.

Mansi—*Sacrorum Conciliorum Nova et Amplissima Collectio*

MGH—Monumenta Germaniae Historica

MPL—Migne, *Patrologia Latina*

S.C.C.—Sacra Congregatio Concilii

S.C. de Prop. Fide—Sacra Congregatio de Propaganda Fide

S.C.S. Off— Suprema Congregatio Sancti Officii

S.C.S.—Sacra Congregatio de Disciplina Sacramentorum

BIOGRAPHICAL NOTE

Robert Bell Clune was born on September 18, 1920, at Toronto, Ontario, Canada. After completing his primary education at St. Vincent de Paul Parochial School, Toronto, he entered St. Michael's College School in the same city. In 1938 he entered St. Augustine's Seminary, Toronto, Ontario, where he received the degree of Bachelor of Arts from St. Michael's College in 1941. He was ordained to the Sacred Priesthood on May 26, 1945. In September of the same year he enrolled in the School of Canon Law at the Catholic University of America, where he received the Degree of the Baccalaureate in Canon Law in June, 1946, and the Degree of the Licentiate in Canon Law the following year.

Law,
  Roman civil, 1.
  Roman criminal, 7.
Libellus, 47, 73, 110.

Medical expert, 106.
Minors, 54.
Moral persons, 54.
Moral certitude, 47, 117.

Notary, 40, 43, 87, 107, 108, 110, 112, 116.

Oaths,
  division of, 78.
  importance of, 80.
  in criminal trials, 35.
  nature of, 77.
  norms for tendering to parties, 80,
  of having spoken the truth, 89, 109, 112.
  of secrecy, 90, 109, 112.
  probative value of, 78.
  procedure in administering, 85.
  refusal to take, 82.
  sanctity of, 43, 86.
  to tell the truth, 20, 35, 40, 52 78, 80, 85, 112.
Object of the interrogations, 49.
Obligation to respond, 29, 37, 113.
Offenses, 52, 55, 83, 94, 100.
Officialis, 63.

Parties,
  right to propose interrogations, 40, 74, 94, 101.
  proof of probity, 43, 104.
  right to have answers recorded verbatim, 109.
Perjury, penalties for, 87, 116.
Personal delicts, 114.
Place for the interrogations, 95.
Plaintiff, interrogation of, 39, 43.
Positiones, 12, 13, 25, 27, 58.

Private good, 53, 81, 83, 101.
Procedure,
  Roman civil law, 1.
  Roman criminal law, 7.
  in early Church, 10.
  in criminal trials, 53, 114, 116.
  in contentious trials, 39.
  in causes of private good, 54.
  in causes of public good, 54, 100.
  for the interrogation, 103.
Procurators, 78, 105, 107, 112.
Promissory oath, 78.
Promoter of justice, 69, 71, 94, 101, 110.
Propositions condemned by Holy Office, 36.
Proxies, 78.
Purpose of interrogations, 47, 91.

Qualities of the interrogations, 72, 91, 113.

Record of the deposition, 116.
Refusal to answer, 14, 116.
Refusal to be sworn, 82, 87.
Regulations of Sacred Roman Rota, 44.
Response of the parties, 108.
Right to interrogate,
  of defender of the bond, 39, 69, 93, 101.
  of judge, 18, 39, 41, 55, 61, 68, 94, 114, 118.
  in causes concerning the private good, 62, 101.
  in causes concerning the public good, 62, 101.
  of parties, 40, 74, 94, 101.
  of promoter of justice, 69, 71, 101.

Time for the interrogations, 98.
Torture,
  Roman law, 8.
  ecclesiastical law, 15, 24.
  the Inquisition, 31.

Vice-officialis, 63, 67.

CANON LAW STUDIES*

1. FRERIKS, REV. CELESTINE A., C.PP.S., J.C.D., Religious Congregations in Their External Relations, 121 pp., 1916.

2. GALLIHER, REV. DANIEL M., O.P., J.C.D., Canonical Elections, 117 pp. 1917.

3. BORKOWSKI, REV. AURELIUS L., O.F.M., J.C.D., De Confraternitatibus Ecclesiasticis, 136 pp., 1918.

4. CASTILLO, REV. CAYO, J.C.D., Disertacion Historico-Canonica sobre la Potestad del Cabildo en Sede Vacante o Impedida del Vicario Capitular, 99 pp., 1919 (1918).

5. KUBELBECK, REV. WILLIAM J., S.T.B.; J.C.D., The Sacred Penitentiaria and Its Relation to Faculties of Ordinaries and Priests, 129 pp., 1918.

6. PETROVITS, REV. JOSEPH J. C., S.T.D., J.C.D., The New Church Law on Matrimony, X-461 pp., 1919.

7. HICKEY, REV. JOHN J., S.T.B., J.C.D., Irregularities and Simple impediments in the New Code of Canon Law, 100 pp., 1920.

8. KLEKOTKA, REV. PETER J., S.T.B., J.C.D., Diocesan Consultors, 179 pp., 1920.

9. WANENMACHER, REV. FRANCIS, J.C.D., The Evidence in Ecclesiastical Procedure Affecting the Marriage Bond, 1920 (Printed 1935).

10. GOLDEN, REV. HENRY FRANCIS, J.C.D., Parochial Benefices in the New Code, IV-119 pp., 1921 (Printed 1925).

11. KOUDELKA, REV. CHARLES J., J.C.D., Pastors, Their Rights and Duties According to the New Code of Canon Law, 211 pp., 1921.

12. MELO, REV. ANTONIUS, O.F.M., J.C.D., De Exemptions Regularium, X-188 pp., 1921.

13. SCHAAF, REV. VALENTINE THEODORE, O.F.M., S.T.B., J.C.D., The Cloister, X-180 pp., 1921.

14. BURKE, REV. THOMAS JOSEPH, S.T.D., J.C.D., Competence in Ecclesiastical Tribunals, IV-117 pp., 1922.

15. LEECH, REV. GEORGE LEO, J.C.D., A Comparative Study of the Constitution "Apostolicae Sedis" and the "Codex Juris Canonici," 179 pp., 1922.

16. MOTRY, REV. HUBERT LOUIS, S.T.D., J.C.D., Diocesan Faculties According to the Code of Canon Law, II-167 pp., 1922.

17. MURPHY, REV. GEORGE LAWRENCE, J.C.D., Delinquencies and Penalties in the Administration and the Reception of the Sacraments, IV-121 pp., 1923.

18. O'REILLY, REV. JOHN ANTHONY, S.T.B., J.C.D., Ecclesiastical Sepulture in the New Code of Canon Law, II-129 pp., 1923.

---

*Below n. 100 only the following numbers are still available: Nn. 3, 4, 9, 25, 34, 57 and 75. Beginning with n. 100 only the following are unavailable: Nn. 100-111 inclusive and n. 113.

19. MICHALICKA, REV. WENCESLAS CYRIL, O.S.B., J.C.D., Judicial Procedure in Dismissal of Clerical Exempt Religious, 107 pp., 1923.
20. DARGIN, REV. EDWARD VINCENT, S.T.B., J.C.D., Reserved Cases According to the Code of Canon Law, IV-103 pp., 1924.
21. GODFREY, REV. JOHN A., S.T.B., J.C.D., The Right of Patronage According to the Code of Canon Law, 153 pp., 1924.
22. HAGEDORN, REV. FRANCIS EDWARD, J.C.D., General Legislation on Indulgences, II-154 pp., 1924.
23. KING, REV. JAMES IGNATIUS, J.C.D., The Administration of the Sacraments to Dying Catholics, V-141 pp., 1924.
24. WINSLOW, REV. FRANCIS JOSEPH, O.F.M., J.C.D., Vicars and Prefects Apostolic, IV-149 pp., 1924.
25. CORREA, REV. JOSE SERVELION, S.T.L., J.C.D., La Potestad Legislativa de la Iglesia Catolica IV-127 pp., 1925.
26. DUGAN, REV. HENRY FRANCIS, A.M., J.C.D., The Judiciary Department of the Diocesan Curia, 87 pp., 1925.
27. KELLER, REV. CHARLES FREDERICK, S.T.B., J.C.D., Mass Stipends, 167 pp., 1925.
28. PASCHANG, REV. JOHN LINUS, J.C.D., The Sacramentals According to the Code of Canon Law, 129 pp., 1925.
29. PIONTEK, REV. CYRILLUS, O.F.M., S.T.B., J.C.D., De Indulto Exclaustrationis necnon Saecularizationis, XIII-289 pp., 1925.
30. KEARNEY, REV. RICHARD JOSEPH, S.T.B., J.C.D., Sponsors at Baptism According to the Code of Canon Law, IV-127 pp., 1925.
31. BARTLETT, REV. CHESTER JOSEPH, A.M., LL.B., J.C.D., The Tenure of Parochial Property in the United States of America, V-108 pp., 1926.
32. KILKER, REV. ADRIAN JEROME, J.C.D., Extreme Unction, V-425 pp., 1926.
33. McCORMICK, REV. ROBERT EMMETT, J.C.D., Confessors of Religious, VIII-266 pp., 1926.
34. MILLER, REV. NEWTON THOMAS, J.C.D., Founded Masses According to the Code of Canon Law, VII-93 pp., 1926.
35. ROELKER, REV. EDWARD G., S.T.D., J.C.D., Principles of Privilege According to the Code of Canon Law, XI-166 pp., 1926.
36. BAKALARCZYK, REV. RICHARDUS, M.I.C., J.U.D., De Novitiatu, VIII-208 pp. 1927.
37. PIZZUTI, REV. LAWRENCE, O.F.M., J.U.L., De Parochis Religiosis, 1927. (Not Printed.)
38. BLILEY, REV. NICHOLAS MARTIN, O.S.B., J.C.D., Altars According to the Code of Canon Law, XIX-132 pp., 1927.
39. BROWN, MR. BRENDAN FRANCIS, A.B., LL.M., J.U.D., The Canonical Juristic Personality with Special Reference to its Status in the United States of America, V-212 pp., 1927.
40. CAVANAUGH, REV. WILLIAM THOMAS, C.P., J.U.D., The Reservation of the Blessed Sacrament, VIII-101 pp., 1927.
41. DOHENY, REV. WILLIAM J., C.S.C., A.B., J.U.D., Church Property: Modes of Acquisition, X-118 pp., 1927.
42. FELDHAUS, REV. ALOYSIUS H., C.PP.S., J.C.D., Oratories, IX-141 pp., 1927.

43. KELLY, REV. JAMES PATRICK, A.B., J.C.D., The Jurisdiction of the Simple Confessor, X-208 pp., 1927.

44. NEUBERGER, REV. NICHOLAS J., J.C.D., Canon 6 or the Relation of the Codex Juris Canonici to the Preceding Legislation, V-95 pp., 1927.

45. O'KEEFE, REV. GERALD MICHAEL, J.C.D., Matrimonial Dispensations, Powers of Bishops, Priests, and Confessors, VIII-232 pp., 1927.

46. QUIGLEY, REV. JOSEPH A. M., A.B., J.C.D., Condemned Societies, 139 pp., 1927.

47. ZAPLOTNIK, REV. JOHANNES LEO, J.C.D., De Vicariis Foraneis, X-142 pp., 1927.

48. DUSKIE, REV. JOHN ALOYSIUS, A.B., J.C.D., The Canonical Status of the Orientals in the United States, VIII-196 pp., 1928.

49. HYLAND, REV. FRANCIS EDWARD, J.C.D., Excommunication, Its Nature, Historical Development and Effects, VIII-181 pp., 1928.

50. REINMANN, REV. GERALD JOSEPH, O.M.C., J.C.D., The Third Order Secular of Saint Francis, 201 pp., 1928.

51. SCHENK, REV. FRANCIS J., J.C.D., The Matrimonial Impediments of Mixed Religion and Disparity of Cult, XVI-318 pp., 1929.

52. COADY, REV. JOHN JOSEPH, S.T.D., J.U.D., A.M., The Appointment of Pastors, VIII-150 pp., 1929.

53. KAY, REV. THOMAS HENRY, J.C.D., Competence in Matrimonial Procedure, VIII-164 pp., 1929.

54. TURNER, REV. SIDNEY JOSEPH, C.P., J.U.D., The Vow of Poverty XLIX-217 pp., 1929.

55. KEARNEY, REV. RAYMOND A., A.B., S.T.D., J.C.D., The Principles of Delegation, VII-149 pp., 1929.

56. CONRAN, REV. EDWARD JAMES, A.B., J.C.D., The Interdict, V-163 pp., 1930.

57. O'NEILL, REV. WILLIAM H., J.C.D., Papal Rescripts of Favor, VII-218 pp., 1930.

58. BASTNAGEL, REV. CLEMENT VINCENT, J.U.D., The Appointment of Parochial Adjutants and Assistants, XV-257 pp., 1930.

59. FERRY, REV. WILLIAM A., A.B., J.C.D., Stole Fees, V-136 pp., 1930.

60. COSTELLO, REV. JOHN MICHAEL, A.B., J.C.D., Domicile and Quasi-Domicile, VII-201 pp., 1930.

61. KREMER, REV. MICHAEL NICHOLAS, A.B., S.T.B., J.C.D., Church Support in the United States, VI-136 pp., 1930.

62. ANGULO, REV. LUIS, C.M., J.C.D., Legislation de la Iglesia sobre la intencion en la application de la Santa Misa, VII-104 pp., 1931.

63. FREY, REV. WOLFGANG NORBERT, O.S.B., A.B., J.C.D., The Act of Religious Profession, VIII-174 pp., 1931.

64. ROBERTS, REV. JAMES BRENDAN, A.B., J.C.D., The Banns of Marriage, XIV-104 pp., 1931.

65. RYDER, REV. RAYMOND ALOYSIUS, A.B., J.C.D., Simony, IX-151 pp., 1931.

66. CAMPAGNA, REV. ANGELO, PH.D., J.U.D., Il Vicario Generale del Vescovo, VII-205 pp., 1931.

67 Cox, Rev. Joseph Godfrey, A.B., J.C.D., The Administration of Seminaries, VI-124 pp., 1931.

68. Gregory, Rev. Donald J., J.U.D., The Pauline Privilege, XV-165 pp., 1931.

69. Donohue, Rev. John F., J.C.D., The Impediment of Crime, VII-110 pp., 1931.

70. Dooley, Rev. Eugene A., O.M.I., J.C.D., Church Law on Sacred Relics IX-143 pp., 1931.

71. Orth, Rev. Clement Raymond, O.M.C., J.C.D., The Approbation of Religious Institutes, 171 pp., 1931.

72. Pernicone, Rev. Joseph M., A.B., J.C.D., The Ecclesiastical Prohibition of Books, XII-267 pp., 1932.

73. Clinton, Rev. Connell, A.B., J.C.D., The Paschal Precept, IX-108 pp., 1932.

74. Donnelly, Rev. Francis B., A.M., S.T.L., J.C.D., The Diocesan Synod, VIII-125 pp., 1932.

75. Torrente, Rev. Camilo, C.M.F., J.C.D., Las Procesiones Sagradas, V-145 pp., 1932.

76. Murphy, Rev. Edwin J., C.PP.S., J.C.D., Suspension Ex Informata Conscientia, XI-122 pp., 1932.

77. MacKenzie, Rev. Eric F., A.M., S.T.L., J.C.D., The Delict of Heresy in its Commission, Penalization, Absolution, VII-124 pp., 1932.

78. Lyons, Rev. Avitus E., S.T.B., J.C.D., The Collegiate Tribunal of First Instance, XI-147 pp., 1932.

79. Connolly, Rev. Thomas A., J.C.D., Appeals, XI-195 pp., 1932.

80. Sangmeister, Rev. Joseph V., A.B., J.C.D., Force and Fear as Precluding Matrimonial Consent, V-211 pp., 1932.

81. Jaeger, Rev. Leo A., A.B., J.C.D., The Administration of Vacant and Quasi-Vacant Episcopal Sees in the United States, IX-229 pp., 1932.

82. Rimlinger, Rev. Herbert T. J.C.D., Error Invalidating Matrimonial Consent, VII-79 pp., 1932.

83. Barrett, Rev. John D. M., S.S., J.C.D., A Comparative Study of the Third Plenary Council of Baltimore and the Code, IX-221 pp., 1932.

84. Carberry, Rev. John J., Ph.D., S.T.D., J.C.D., The Juridical Form of Marriage, X-177 pp., 1934.

85. Dolan, Rev. John L., A.B., J.C.D., The Defensor Vinculi, XII-157 pp., 1934.

86. Hannan, Rev. Jerome D., A.M., S.T.D., LL.B., J.C.D., The Canon Law of Wills, IX-517 pp., 1934.

87. Lemieux, Rev. Delise A., A.M., J.C.D., The Sentence in Ecclesiastical Procedure, IX-131 pp., 1934.

88. O'Rourke, Rev. James J., A.B., J.C.D., Parish Registers, VII-109 pp., 1934.

89. Timlin, Rev. Bartholomew, O.F.M., A.M., J.C.D., Conditional Matrimonial Consent, X-381 pp., 1934.

90. Wahl, Rev. Francis X., A.B., J.C.D., The Matrimonial Impediments of Consanguinity and Affinity, VI-125 pp., 1934.

91. WHITE, REV. ROBERT J., A.B., LL.B., S.T.B., J.C.D., Canonical Ante-Nuptial Promises and the Civil Law, VI-152 pp., 1934.

92. HERRERA, REV. ANTONIO PARRA, O.C.D., J.C.D., Legislacion Ecclesiastica sobra el Ayuno y la Abstinencia, XI-191 pp., 1935.

93. KENNEDY, REV. EDWIN J., J.C.D., The Special Matrimonial Process in Cases of Evident Nullity, X-165 pp., 1935.

94. MANNING, REV. JOHN J., A.B., J.C.D., Presumption of Law in Matrimonial Procedure, XI-111 pp., 1935.

95. MOEDER, REV. JOHN M., J.C.D., The Proper Bishop for Ordination and Dimissorial Letters, VII-135 pp., 1935.

96. O'MARA, REV. WILLIAM A., A.B., J.C.D., Canonical Causes for Matrimonial Dispensations, IX-155 pp., 1935.

97. REILLY, REV. PETER, J.C.D., Residence of Pastors, IX-81 pp., 1935.

98. SMITH, REV. MARINER T., O.P., S.T.Lr., J.C.D., The Penal Law for Religious, VII-169 pp., 1935.

99. WHALEN, REV. DONALD W., A.M., J.C.D., The Value of Testimonial Evidence in Matrimonial Procedure, XIII-297 pp., 1935.

100. CLEARY, REV. JOSEPH F., J.C.D., Canonical Limitations on the Alienation of Church Property, VIII-141 pp., 1936.

101. GLYNN, REV. JOHN C., J.C.D., The Promoter of Justice, XX-337 pp., 1936.

102. BRENNAN, REV. JAMES H., S.S., M.A., S.T.B., J.C.D., The Simple Convalidation of Marriage, VI-135 pp., 1937.

103. BUNINI, REV. JOSEPH BERNARD, J.C.D., The Clerical Obligations of Canons 139 and 142, X-121 pp., 1937.

104. CONNOR, REV. MAURICE, A.B., J.C.D,. The Administrative Removal of Pastors, VIII-159 pp., 1937.

105. GUILFOYLE, REV. MERLIN JOSEPH, J.C.D., Custom, XI-144 pp., 1937.

106. HUGHES, REV. JAMES AUSTIN, A.B., A.M., J.C.D., Witnesses in Criminal Trials of Clerics, IX-140 pp., 1937.

107. JANSEN, REV. RAYMOND J., A.B., S.T.L., J.C.D., Canonical Provisions for Catechetical Instruction, VII-153 pp., 1937.

108. KEALY, REV. JOHN JAMES, A.B., J.C.D., The Introductory Libellus in Church Court Procedure, XI-121 pp., 1937.

109. McMANUS, REV. JAMES EDWARD, C.SS.R., J.C.D., The Administration of Temporal Goods in Religious Institutes, XVI-196 pp., 1937.

110. MORIARTY, REV. EUGENE JAMES, J.C.D., Oaths in Ecclesiastical Courts, X-115 pp., 1937.

111. RAINER, REV. ELIGIUS GEORGE, C.SS.R., J.C.D., Suspension of Clerics, XVII-249 pp., 1937.

112. REILLY, REV. THOMAS F., C.SS.R., J.C.D., Visitation of Religious, VI-195 pp., 1938.

113. MORIARITY, REV. FRANCIS E., C.SS.R., J.C.D., The Extraordinary Absolution from Censures, XV-334 pp., 1938.

114. CONNOLLY, REV. NICHOLAS P., J.C.D., The Canonical Erection of Parishes, X-132 pp., 1938.

115. DONOVAN, REV. JAMES JOSEPH, J.C.D., The Pastor's Obligation in Prenuptial Investigation, XII-322 pp., 1938.

116. HARRIGAN, REV. ROBERT J., M.A., S.T.B., J.C.D., The Radical Sanation of Invalid Marriages, XII-236 pp., 1939.

117. BOFFA, REV. CONRAD HUMBERT, J.C.D., Canonical Provisions for Catholic Schools, VII-211 pp., 1939.

118. PARSONS, REV. ANSCAR JOHN, O.M.Cap., J.C.D., Canonical Elections, XII-236 pp., 1939.

119. REILLY, REV. EDWARD MICHAEL, A.B., J.C.D., The General Norms of Dispensation, XII-156 pp., 1939.

120. RYAN, REV. GERALD ALOYSIUS, A.B., J.C.D., Principles of Episcopal Jurisdiction, XII-172 pp., 1939.

121. BURTON, REV. FRANCIS JAMES, C.S.C., A.B., J.C.D. A Commentary on Canon 1125, X-222 pp., 1940.

122. MIASKIEWICZ, REV. FRANCIS SIGISMUND, J.C.D., Supplied Jurisdiction According to Canon 209, XII-340 pp., 1940.

123. RICE, REV. PATRICK WILLIAM, A.B., J.C.D., Proof of Death in Prenuptial Investigation, VIII-156 pp., 1940.

124. ANGLIN, REV. THOMAS FRANCIS, M.S., J.C.D., The Eucharistic Fast, VIII-183 pp., 1941.

125. COLEMAN, REV. JOHN JEROME, J.C.D., The Minister of Confirmation, VI-153 pp., 1941.

126. DOWNS, REV. JOSEPH EMMANUEL, A.B., J.C.D., The Concept of Clerical Immunity, XI-163 pp., 1941.

127. ESSWEIN, REV. ANTHONY ALBERT, J.C.D., Extrajudicial Penal Powers of Ecclesiastical Superiors, X-144 pp., 1941.

128. FARRELL, REV. BENJAMIN FRANCIS, M.A., S.T.L., J.C.D., The Rights and Duties of the Local Ordinary Regarding Congregations of Women Religious of Pontifical Approval, V-195 pp., 1941.

129. FEENEY, REV. THOMAS JOHN, A.B., S.T.L., J.C.D., Restitutio in Integrum, VI-169 pp., 1941.

130. FINDLAY, REV. STEPHEN WILLIAM, O.S.B., A.B., J.C.D., Canonical Norms Governing the Deposition and Degradation of Clerics, XVII-279 pp., 1941.

131. GOODWINE, REV. JOHN, A.B., S.T.L., J.C.D., The Right of the Church to Acquire Property, VIII-119 pp., 1941.

132. HESTON, REV. EDWARD LOUIS, C.S.C., PH.D., S.T.D., J.C.D., The Alienation of Church Property in the United States, XII-222 pp., 1941.

133. HOGAN, REV. JAMES JOHN, A.B., S.T.L., J.C.D., Judicial Advocates and Procurators, XIII-200 pp., 1941.

134. KEALY, REV. THOMAS M., A.B., LITT.D., J.C.D., Dowry of Women Religious, IX-152 pp., 1941.

135. KEENE, REV. MICHAEL JAMES, O.S.B., J.C.D., Religious Ordinaries and Canon 198, V-164 pp., 1942.

136. KERIN, REV. CHARLES A., S.S., M.A., S.T.B., J.C.D., The Privation of Christian Burial, XVI-279 pp., 1941.

137. LOUIS, REV. WILLIAM FRANCIS, M.A., J.C.D., Diocesan Archives, X-101 pp., 1941.

138. McDEVITT, REV. GILBERT JOSEPH, A.B., J.C.D., Legitimacy and Legitimation, X-247 pp., 1941.

139. McDONOUGH, REV. THOMAS JOSEPH, A.B., J.C.D., Apostolic Administrators, X-217 pp., 1941.

140. MEIER, REV. CARL ANTHONY, A.B., J.C.D., Penal Administration Procedure Against Negligent Pastors, XI-240 pp., 1941.

141. SCHMIDT, REV. JOHN ROGG, A.B., J.C.D., The Principles of Authentic Interpretation in Canon 17 of the Code of Canon Law, XII-331 pp., 1941.

142. SLAFKOSKY, REV. ANDREW LEONARD, A.B., J.C.D., The Canonical Episcopal Visitation of the Diocese, X-197 pp., 1941.

143. SWOBODA, REV. INNOCENT ROBERT, O.F.M., J.C.D., Ignorance in Relation to the Imputability of Delicts, IX-271 pp., 1941.

144. DUBE, REV. ARTHUR JOSEPH, A.B., J.C.D., The General Principles for the Reckoning of Time in Canon Law, VIII-299 pp., 1941.

145. McBRIDE, REV. JAMES T., A.B., J.C.D., Incardination and Excardination of Seculars, XX-585 pp., 1941.

146. KROL, REV. JOHN T., J.C.D., The Defendant in Ecclesiastical Trials, XII-207 pp., 1942.

147. COMYNS, REV. JOSEPH J., C.SS.R., A.B., J.C.D., Papal and Episcopal Administration of Church Property, XIV-155 pp., 1942.

148. BARRY, REV. GARRETT FRANCIS, O.M.I., J.C.D., Violation of the Cloister, XII-260 pp., 1942.

149. BOLDUC, REV. GATIEN, C.S.V., A.B., S.T.L., J.C.D., Les Etudes dans les Religions Cléricales, VIII-155 pp., 1942.

150. BOYLE, REV. DAVID JOHN, M.A., J.C.D., The Juridic Effects of Moral Certitude on Pre-Nuptial Guarantees, XII-188 pp., 1942.

151. CANAVAN, REV. WALTER JOSEPH, M.A., LITT.D., J.C.D., The Profession of Faith, XII-143 pp., 1942.

152. DESROCHERS, REV. BRUNO, A.B., PH.L., S.T.B., J.C.D., Le Premier Concile Plénier de Québec et le Code de Droit Canonique, XIV-186 pp., 1942.

153. DILLON, REV. ROBERT EDWARD, A.B., J.C.D., Common Law Marriage, X-148 pp., 1942.

154. DODWELL, REV. EDWARD JOHN, PH.D., S.T.B., J.C.D., The Time and Place for the Celebration of Marriage, X-156 pp., 1942.

155. DONNELLAN, REV. THOMAS ANDREW, A.B., J.C.D., The Obligation of the Missa pro Populo, VII-131 pp., 1942.

156. ELTZ, REV. LOUIS ANTHONY, A.B., J.C.L., Cooperation in Crime.

157. GASS, REV. SYLVESTER FRANCIS, M.A., J.C.D., Ecclesiastical Pensions, XI-206 pp., 1942.

158. GUINIVEN, REV. JOHN JOSEPH, C.SS.R., J.C.D., The Precept of Hearing Mass, XIV-188 pp., 1942.

159. GULCZYNSKI, REV. JOHN THEOPHILUS, J.C.D., The Desecration and Violation of Churches, X-126 pp., 1942.

160. HAMMILL, REV. JOHN LEO, M.A. J.C.D., The Obligations of the Traveler According to Canon 14, VIII-204 pp., 1942.

161. HAYDT, REV. JOHN JOSEPH, A.B., J.C.D., Reserved Benefices, XI-148 pp., 1942.

162 HUSHER, REV. ROGER JOHN, O.F.M., A.B., J.C.D., The Crime of Abortion in Canon Law, XII-187 pp., 1942.

163. KEARNEY, REV. FRANCIS PATRICK, A.B., S.T.L., J.C.L., The Principles of Canon 1127.

164. LINAHEN, REV. LEO JAMES, S.T.L., J.C.D., De Absolutione Complicis In Peccato Turpi, 114 pp., 1942.

165. McCLOSKEY, REV. JOSEPH ALOYSIUS, A.B., J.C.D., The Subject of Ecclesiastical Law According to Canon 12, XVII-246 pp., 1942.

166. O'NEILL, REV. FRANCIS JOSEPH, C.SS.R., J.C.D., The Dismissal of Religious in Temporary Vows, XIII-220 pp., 1942.

167. PRINCE, REV. JOHN EDWARD, A.B., S.T.D., J.C.D., The Diocesan Chancellor, X-136 pp., 1942.

168. RIESNER, REV. ALBERT JOSEPH, C.SS.R., J.C.D., Apostates and Fugitives from Religious Institutes, IX-168 pp., 1942.

169. STENGER, REV. JOSEPH BERNARD, J.C.D., The Mortgaging of Church Property, 186 pp., 1942.

170. WALDRON, REV. JOSEPH FRANCIS, A.B., J.C.D., The Minister of Baptism, XII-197 pp., 1942.

171. WILLETT, REV. ROBERT ALBERT, J.C.D., The Probative Value of Documents in Ecclesiastical Trials, X-124 pp., 1942.

172. WOEBER, REV. EDWARD MARTIN, M.A., J.C.D., The Interpellations, XII-161 pp., 1942.

173. BENKO, REV. MATTHEW ALOYSIUS, O.S.B., M.A., J.C.L., The Abbot *Nullius.*

174. CHRIST, REV. JOSEPH JAMES, M.A., S.T.L., J.C.L., Dispensation from Vindicative Penalties.

175. CLANCY, REV. PATRICK M. J., O.P., A.B., S.T.Lr., J.C.D., The Local Religious Superior, X-299 pp., 1943.

176. CLARKE, REV. THOMAS JAMES, J.C.D., Parish Societies, XII-147 pp., 1943.

177. CONNOLLY, REV. JOHN PATRICK, S.T.L., J.C.D., Synodal Examiners and Parish Priest Consultors, X-223 pp., 1943.

178. DRUMM, REV. WILLIAM MARTIN, A.B., J.C.L., Hospital Chaplains.

179. FLANAGAN, REV. BERNARD JOSEPH, A.B., S.T.L., J.C.D., The Canonical Erection of Religious Houses, X-147 pp., 1943.

180. KELLEHER, REV. STEPHEN JOSEPH, A.B., S.T.B., J.C.D., Discussions with non-Catholics: Canonical Legislation, X-93 pp., 1943.

181. LEWIS, REV. GORDIAN, C.P., J.C.D., Chapters in Religious Institutes, XII-169 pp., 1943.

182. MARX, REV. ADOLPH, J.C.D., The Declaration of Nullity of Marriages Contracted Outside the Church, X-151 pp., 1943.

183. MATULENAS, REV. RAYMOND ANTHONY, O.S.B., A.B., J.C.L., Communication, a Source of Privileges.

184. O'LEARY, REV. CHARLES GERARD, C.SS.R., J.C.D., Religious Dismissed After Perpetual Profession, X-213 pp., 1943.

185. POWER, REV. CORNELIUS MICHAEL, J.C.L., The Blessing of Cemeteries.

186. SHUHLER, REV. RALPH VINCENT, O.S.A., J.C.D., Privileges of Regulars to Absolve and Dispense, XII-195 pp., 1943.

187. ZIOLKOWSKI, REV. THADDEUS STANISLAUS, A.B., J.C.D., The Consecration and Blessing of Churches, XII-151 pp., 1943.

188. HENEGHAN, REV. JOHN JOSEPH, S.T.D., J.C.L., The Marriages of Unworthy Catholics: Canons 1065 and 1066.

189. CARROLL, REV. COLEMAN FRANCIS, M.A., S.T.L., J.C.L., Charitable Institutions.

190. CIESLUK, REV. JOSEPH EDWARD, Ph.B., S.T.L., J.C.L., National Parishes in the United States.

191. COBURN, REV. VINCENT PAUL, A.B., J.C.L., Marriages of Conscience.

192. CONNORS, REV. CHARLES PAUL, C.S.Sp., A.B., J.C.L., Extra-Judicial Procurators in the Code of Canon Law.

193. COYLE, REV. PAUL RAYMOND, A.B., J.C.L., Judicial Exceptions.

194. FAIR, REV. BARTHOLOMEW FRANCIS, A.B., S.T.L., J.C.L., The Impediment of Abduction.

195. GALLAGHER, REV. THOMAS RAPHAEL, O.P., A.B., S.T.Lr., J.C.L., The Examination of the Qualities of the Ordinand.

196. GANNON, REV. JOHN MARK, S.T.L., J.C.L., The Interstices Required for the Promotion to Orders.

197. GOLDSMITH, REV. J. WILLIAM, B.C.S., S.T.L., J.C.L., The Competence of Church and State over Marriage—Disputed Points.

198. GOODWINE, REV. JOSEPH GERARD, A.B., S.T.B., J.C.L., The Reception of Converts.

199. KOWALSKI, REV. ROMUALD, EUGENE, O.F.M., A.B., J.C.L., Sustenance of Religious Houses of Regulars.

200. McCOY, REV. ALAN EDWARD, O.F.M., J.C.L., Force and Fear in Relation to Delictual Imputability and Penal Responsibility.

201. McDEVITT, REV. VINCENT JOHN, Ph.B., S.T.L., J.C.L., Perjury.

202. MARTIN, REV. THOMAS OWEN, Ph.D., S.T.D., J.C.L., Adverse Possession, Prescription and Limitation of Actions: The Canonical "Praescriptio."

203. MIKLOSOVIC, REV. PAUL JOHN, A.B., J.C.L., Attempted Marriages and Their Consequent Juridic Effects.

204. MUNDY, REV. THOMAS MAURICE, A.B., S.T.L., J.C.L., The Union of Parishes.

205. O'DEA, REV. JOHN COYLE, A.B., J.C.L., The Matrimonial Impediment of Nonage.

206. OLALIA, REV. ALEXANDER AYSON, S.T.L., J.C.L., A Comparative Study of the Christian Constitution of States and the Constitution of the Philippine Commonwealth.

207. POISSON, REV. PIERRE-MARIE, C.S.C., A.B., Ph.L., Th.L., J.C.L., Droits Patrimoniaux des Maisons et des Eglises Religieuses.

208. STADALNIKAS, REV. CASIMIR JOSEPH, M.I.C., J.C.L., Reservation of Censures.

209. SULLIVAN, REV. EUGENE HENRY, S.T.L., J.C.L., Proof of the Reception of the Sacraments.

210. VAUGHAN, REV. WILLIAM EDWARD, J.C.L., Constitutions for Diocesan Courts.

211. PARO, REV. GINO, S.T.D., J.C.L., The Right of Apostolic Legation.

212. BALZER, REV. RALPH FRANCIS, C.P., J.C.L., The Computation of Time in a Canonical Novitiate.

213. DOUGHERTY, REV. JOHN WHELAN, A.B., S.T.L., J.C.L., De Inquisitione Speciali.

214. Dziob, Rev. Michael Walter, J.C.L., The Sacred Congregation for the Oriental Church.

215. Eidenschink, Rev. John Albert, O.S.B., B.A., J.C.L., The Election of Bishops in the Letters of Pope Gregory the Great.

216. Gill, Rev. Nicholas, C.P., J.C.L., The Spiritual Prefect in Clerical Religious Houses of Study.

217. Hynes, Rev. Harry Gerard, S.T.L., J.C.D., The Privileges of Cardinals, XII-183 pp., 1945.

218. McDevitt, Rev. Gerard Vincent, S.T.L., J.C.D., The Renunciation of an Ecclesiastical Office, XIV—179 pp., 1946.

219. Manning, Rev. Joseph Leroy, J.C.L., The Free Conferral of Offices.

220. Meyer, Rev. Louis G., O.S.B., A.B., S.T.B., J.C.D., Alms-Gathering by Religious, XII—163 pp., 1946.

221. O'Donnell, Rev. Cletus Francis, M.A., J.C.D., The Marriage of Minors, XII-268 pp., 1945.

222. Prunskis, Rev. Joseph, J.C.D., Comparative Law, Ecclesiastical and Civil, in Lithuanian Concordat, X-161 pp., 1945.

223. Sweeney, Rev. Francis Patrick, C.SS.R., J.C.D., The Reduction of Clerics to the Lay State, X-199 pp., 1945.

224. Vogelpohl, Rev. Henry John, J.C.D., The Simple Impediments to Holy Orders, XVI-190 pp., 1945.

225. Brockhaus, Rev. Thomas Aquinas, O.S.B., J.C.D., Religious Who Are Known as *Conversi*, X-127 pp., 1945.

226. Griese, Rev. N. Orville, S.T.D., J.C.D., The Marriage Contract and the Procreation of Offspring, XVI-224 pp., 1946.

227. Boudreaux, Rev. Warren Louis, J.C.D., The *"ab acatholicis nati"* of Canon 1099, § 2, XII-110 pp., 1946.

228. Bowe, Rev. Thomas Joseph, A.B., J.C.D., Religious Superioresses, VIII-206 pp., 1946.

229. Diederichs, Rev. Michael Ferdinand, S.C.J., J.C.D., The Jurisdiction of the Latin Ordinaries Over Their Oriental Subjects, XIV-153 pp., 1946.

230. Dingman, Rev. Maurice John, A.B., S.T.L. J.C.L., The Plaintiff in Contentious Trials.

231. Frison, Rev. Basil, C.M.F., M.Mus., J.C.D., The Retroactivity of Law, X-221 pp., 1946.

232. Galvin, Rev. William Anthony, M.A., J.C.D., The Administrative Transfer of Pastors, XII-288 pp., 1946.

233. Goracy, Rev. Joseph C., J.C.L., The Diriment Matrimonial Impediment of Major Orders.

234. Hale, Rev. Joseph Francis, M.A., S.T.L., J.C.L., The Pastor of Burial.

235. Henry, Rev. Joseph Arthur, A.B., J.C.D., The Mass and Holy Communion: Inter-Ritual Law, XII-138 pp., 1946.

236. Linenberger, Rev. Herbert, C.PP.S., J.C.L., The False Denunciation of an Innocent Confessor.

237. Lowry, Rev. James Martin, A.B., J.C.D., Dispensation from Private Vows, XII-266 pp., 1946.

238. LYNCH, REV. GEORGE EDWARD, A.B., S.T.L., J.C.D., Coadjutors and Auxiliaries of Bishops, X-107 pp., 1947.

239. LYNCH, REV. TIMOTHY, M.S.SS.T., J.C.D., Contracts Between Bishops and Religious Congregations, XIV-232 pp., 1946.

240. McCLUNN, REV. JUSTIN DAVID, A.B., S.T.L., J.C.D., Administrative Recourse, VII-142 pp., 1946.

241. LOHMULLER, REV. MARTIN NICHOLAS, A.B., J.C.D., The Promulgation of Law, XII-140 pp., 1947.

242. McGRATH, REV. JAMES, A.B., J.C.D., The Privilege of the Canon, XII-156 pp., 1946.

243. MARBACH, REV. JOSEPH FRANCIS, A.B., J.C.D., Marriage Legislation for the Catholics of the Oriental Rites in the United States and Canada, XIV-314 pp., 1946.

244. SHIMKUS, REV. BERNARD ALOYSIUS, A.B., J.C.L., The Determination and Transfer of Rite.

245. SMITH, REV. VINCENT MICHAEL, A.B., S.T.L., J.C.L., Ignorance Affecting Matrimonial Consent.

246. WACHTELE, REV. PAUL ANTHONY, A.B., J.C.L., The Baptism of the Children of Non-Catholics.

247. CROTTY, REV. MATTHEW MICHAEL, J.C.D., The Recipient of First Holy Communion, X-142 pp., 1947.

248. EAGLETON, REV. GEORGE, J.C.L., The Quinquennial Faculties, Formula IV.

249. GIBBONS, REV. MARION LEO, C.M., LL.B., J.C.D., Domicile of the Wife Unlawfully Separated from Her Husband, XIV-171 pp.. 1947.

250. KELLY, REV. BERNARD MATTHEW, S.T.L., J.C.D., The Functions Reserved to Pastors, XII-141 pp., 1947.

251. KILCULLEN, REV. THOMAS JOHN, LL.M., J.C.D., The Collegiate Moral Person as Party Litigant, X-150 pp., 1947.

252. LAFONTAINE, REV. GERMAIN JOSEPH, W.F., J.C.L., Relations Canoniques entre le Missionnaire et Ses Superieurs.

253. LANE, REV. LORAS THOMAS, A.B., S.T.L., J.C.L., Matrimonial Procedure in the Ordinary Court of Second Instance.

254. LOVER, REV. JAMES FRANCIS, C.SS.R., J.C.D., The Master of Novices, X-168 pp., 1947.

255. McNICHOLAS, REV. TIMOTHY JOSEPH, J.C.L., The *Septimae Manus* Witness.

256. MAROSITZ, REV. JOSEPH JOHN, M.S.C., J.C.D., Obligations and Privileges of Religious Promoted to the Episcopal or Cardinalatial Dignities, XII-180 pp., 1947.

257. MURPHY, REV. FRANCIS JOSEPH, A.B., J.C.D., Legislative Powers of the Provincial Council, XII-158 pp., 1947.

258. O'BRIEN, REV. ROMAEUS WILLIAM, O.CARM., J.C.D., The Provincial Superior in Religious Orders of Men, X-294 pp., 1947.

259. PFALLER, REV. BENEDICT AUGUSTINE, O.S.B., J.C.L., The *Ipso Facto* Effected Dismissal of Religious.

260. POPEK, REV. ALPHONSE SYLVESTER, M.A., J.C.D., The Rights and Obligations of Metropolitans, XVIII-460 pp., 1947.

261. RISTUCCIA, REV. BERNARD JOSEPH, C.M., J.C.L., Quasi-Religious.

262. SONNTAG, REV. NATHANIEL LOUIS, O.F.M.Cap., J.C.D., Censorship of Special Classes of Books, XII-147 pp., 1947.

263. STADLER, REV. JOSEPH NICHOLAS, J.C.L., Frequent Holy Communion.

264. SZAL, REV. IGNATIUS JOSEPH, J.C.L., The Communication of Catholics with Schismatics.

265. WAGNER, REV. URBAN STANLEY, O.F.M.Conv., J.C.D., Parochial Substitute Vicars and Supplying Priests, X-126 pp., 1947.

266. QUINN, REV. JOSEPH, M.A., J.C.L., Documents Required for the Reception of Orders.

267. BENNINGTON, REV. JAMES CLEMENT, A.B., J.C.L., The Recipient of Confirmation.

268. BLAHER, REV. DAMIAN JOSEPH, O.F.M., A.B., J.C.L., The Ordinary Processes in Causes of Beatification and Canonization.

269. CLUNE, REV. ROBERT BELL, B.A., J.C.L. Judicial Interrogation of the Parties.

270. COURTEMANCHE, REV. BASIL F., B.A., J.C.L., The Total Simulation of Matrimonial Consent.

271. DLOUHY, REV. MAUR JOHN, O.S.B. A,B., J.C.L., The Ordination of Exempt Religious.

272. DONOVAN, REV. JOHN THOMAS, PH.B., S.T.L., J.C.L., The Clerical Obligations of Canons 138 and 140.

273. FREKING, REV. FREDERICK W., A.B., S.T.B., J.C.L., The Canonical Installation of Pastors.

274. FULTON, REV. THOMAS B., J.C.L., Prenuptial Investigation.

275. GODLEY, REV. JAMES P., J.C.L. The Time and the Place for the Celebration of Mass.

276. KANE, REV. THOMAS A., A.B., B.S., J.C.L., Jurisdiction of Patriarchs until 1439.

277. KENNEDY, REV. ANDREW A., J.C.L., The Annual Pastoral Report to the Local Ordinary.

278. KONRAD, REV. JOSEPH GEORGE, J.C.L., Transfer of Religious.

279. KRESS, REV. ALPHONSE, J.C.L., Contumacy in Ecclesiastical Trials.

280. McCARTNEY, REV. MARCELLUS ANTHONY, O.F.M., M.A., J.C.L., Faculties of Regular Confessors.

281. McCASLIN, REV. EDWARD PATRICK, M.A., S.T.L., J.C.L., The Division of Parishes.

282. McELROY, REV. FRANCIS J., A.B., J.C.L., The Privileges of Bishops.

283. QUINN, REV. STEPHEN. M.S.SS.T., J.C.L., Relation between the Local Ordinary and Religious of Diocesan Approval.

284. SCHNEIDER, REV. EDELHARD LOUIS, S.D.S., M.A., J.C.L., The Status of Secularized Ex-Religious Clerics.

285. THOMPSON, REV. CHESTER J., A.B., J.C.L., The Simple Removal from Office.

Printed in the USA
CPSIA information can be obtained
at www.ICGtesting.com
LVHW041628301223
767084LV00016B/242